Family Circle

CHILDREN'S PARTIES

IDEAS ★ THEMES ★ RECIPES

★ JUDY WILLIAMS ★

HAMLYN

First published in 1992.
Hamlyn is an imprint of
Octopus Illustrated Books
Michelin House,
81 Fulham Road,
London SW3 6RB

Copyright © Reed International Books Limited 1992

ISBN 0 600 57564 0 (hardback)

ISBN 0 600 57606 X (paperback)

A catalogue record for this book
is available from the British Library

Produced by Mandarin Offset
Printed and bound in Hong Kong

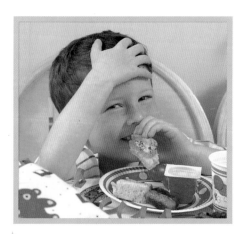

CONTENTS

PLANNING A PARTY

Children always look forward to a birthday party, especially if it is their own. However, parents do not always feel the same way. For first-timers there can be a sense of dread and uncertainty, whereas those who are having their umpteenth party might be running out of ideas. This book will come to your rescue! Packed full of practical information, as well as ideas for cakes, food and games, it covers every aspect of giving a successful children's party.

PLANNING AHEAD

There are lots of things to think about before throwing a children's party to ensure that it all runs smoothly and everyone, including you, enjoys themselves. Going to parties is one of the stages in the development of children's social skills – they learn to mix and play with others, how to behave away from a parent and how to cope on their own in difficult situations. At the parties you give you will spot the natural leader who likes to organize and help a lot, and the shyer, quieter child who needs to join in when he or she is ready and is quite happy playing alone. A good mix of both types makes for a good party so don't just ask all the noisy ones, thinking the party will go with more of a swing. And there are also lots of practical things to think about, too...

Can I afford it?

Food can be provided fairly cheaply for younger children as they tend just to nibble. Older children expect more food so ask fewer of them if this will be a problem. It is also much cheaper to make things yourself rather than buy ready-prepared food. Have plenty of drinks, though, as children get very thirsty playing hectic games. Taking older kids out will obviously be more expensive. There are professional entertainers who will keep them busy for a couple of hours, at a price. The children will enjoy themselves just as much if you organize simple food, like hot dogs and oven chips, followed by ice-cream and games they enjoy.

How many guests?

This does depend on the age of the children but as a general rule keep the numbers fairly small – don't aim for more than 12. Numbers also depend on who your child would like to attend: they may want to ask their whole class or just a few best friends, but a compromise can usually be reached. Don't be bullied into taking on more children than you can manage or afford. You can always ask friends to help. Don't forget that very small children will be accompanied by their mums who will probably require at least a cup of tea, so numbers will be doubled.

When to have it?

Pre-school children are available most afternoons for a party, but consider the parents that may have to pick up older children from school. School-age children are usually happier having parties at weekends when they probably have more free time. Check with parents to make sure the best friends are available on the decided date to avoid serious disappointment. If your child's birthday is during school holidays, try to make sure he or she does not miss out, by holding the party before term ends or after the new term starts. Give out the invitations in good time. Make sure the children wear appropriate clothes: for outdoor parties, scruffier older clothes are obviously more suitable, whereas favourite party clothes can be worn for indoor parties.

How long should it last?

Keep it short. Much better to finish when everyone is having a good time and before they reach the arguing stage! About 1½ -2 hours is usually

long enough, especially for younger children as they can get fractious. This allows enough time to greet guests, open presents, play games, eat and play a few more games before it's time to go. If you are taking them out they will be in your care longer.

Do I need help?

The answer is yes. Ask your partner if possible but otherwise ask friends or relatives to stay so you can work as a team. It is almost impossible to organize and supervise the games, and prepare and serve food at the same time; even if you can manage it, you only need one unhappy child and you'll be tearing your hair out! If you are having a toddlers' party, ask the parents to help as well. Small children need much more looking after and supervision than older ones. They'll be climbing stairs, emptying shelves and asking for the toilet all at the same time! It'll be enough to put you off having another party again! Ask a friend to take photos for you. You will

be too busy and it would be a shame not to have any to look at later.

Do I need invitations?

Receiving an invitation is always exciting for a child. You can use invitations to set the theme of the party and help build up eager anticipation. Buy them or make your own to suit the party. There are lots of ideas for invitations throughout this book. Ask your guests to reply to the invitation so you have definite numbers to cater for. Young children given invitations at school have a habit of losing them so if you haven't heard from someone in particular, it is probably a good idea to contact the parent to check the invite was received. Give invitations out in plenty of time, especially if the birthday party is to be held during a school holiday.

What sort of food?

This rather depends where you are having the party and how old the guests are. The general rule, however, is to keep it simple. Don't slave away over a hot oven for ages; children are very fussy eaters and it's best to prepare something you know most children like. If the party is outside, you don't need to worry about the mess made from crumbs and spillages, but if you are using your lounge or dining room, don't serve food that could spoil your furniture. For toddlers, have finger food that isn't too messy as they will probably eat on the move. If you are cooking a simple meal like hot dogs and oven chips, make sure the children all sit at the table. Older children like buffets, where they can help themselves and can stay in small groups to talk. (If they're at that awkward age, it also

Make the birthday cake the centrepiece of the tea table when laying out the party food. Afterall, it has probably taken a lot of time and effort to create.

Kids like to eat with their fingers, so choose food that won't make too much mess and supply paper containers.

saves the embarrassment of sitting next to a member of the opposite sex!) But accidents are bound to happen so be prepared: don't fill glasses too full, use paper plates and have a damp cloth handy. Check none of the guests is on a special diet. If they are, try and make them something similar to the others so they don't feel excluded. Ask their parents for advice or to supply something suitable.

Should I have prizes?

Most children are very competitive and like to win prizes. This can cause friction and arguments so it's best to make sure everyone wins something. A game like Pass the Parcel can have a small gift under each layer of paper and with careful management of the music it's possible to make certain that everyone, including the birthday child, gets a prize.

For other games have a basket of sweets or small tokens so the winner, and then everyone else, can choose something when the game is over. Or, let the winner start the next game, get their tea first or pick a team rather than receive an actual prize. Lots of

The other guests will enjoy watching the birthday child open his presents. It helps to create a party atmosphere.

parents feel under pressure to send each child home with a party bag as well. This is a personal choice but be warned – it can be very expensive to fill! A balloon, a piece of cake and a box of sweets is quite adequate.

What about opening presents?

Anyone who has spent time and trouble choosing a present likes to see their friend open it. If possible, presents should be opened on the day, but if the recipient is over-whelmed with them, he or she will probably rip each one open quickly in order to rush on to the next, without really noticing the gift. Try to make sure this doesn't happen. Keep a list of who gave each present so your child can write and thank the givers properly afterwards.

Indoors or outdoors?

This depends on whether you have access to a garden and the weather – the one thing that you can never be certain about! If at all possible, it's always best to use some outside space in order to avoid a mess indoors and so that activities can be organized in more space and different games can

be played. Toddlers especially like to play outside (such as in a sand pit). If they have more space to move around in, they will annoy each other less! But check carefully that your garden is childproof – no holes in fences or easy-to-open gates. If you have a pond or pool, make sure they cannot fall in. And, most importantly, make sure there are no poisonous plants or seeds within easy reach.

What about helpers?

Make sure you cater for any adults who are helping: they are at the party too and may not like Marmite fingers! Lay on drinks and adult food for them, on a table out of the children's reach. They will enjoy the party much more if they feel included.

Should I put up decorations?

To give the house a real party feel, it's a good idea to put up some decorations, even if they're only balloons. If you are having a theme party, there are additional suggestions

in the next section. Streamers made from crêpe paper and cards on shelves all help the party mood. Hang some balloons outside the house so the guests know where to come.

What about the mess?

Excitable children rushing about are bound to knock each other and your precious possessions over, so put away anything valuable. Don't worry about cleaning the house beforehand – they will make more mess so it's a waste of time! Restrict the children's space, explain to them that any room with the door shut is out of bounds. Put a gate at the bottom of the stairs to prevent toddlers disappearing. Put away any of your children's favourite toys so they can't be played with and fought over. Children often discard toys they have finished playing with and they can easily get trodden on or broken. Push furniture up against the walls and move any lamps. Take any

keys out of doors and check they can use the lock on the bathroom door without shutting themselves in for the duration of the party.

Should we take them out?

If you choose to have the party at a restaurant or fast-food chain, you will have to consider the restrictions that places on you in terms of transport and numbers. You will need help with young children, who tend to run riot and get rather over-excited, but otherwise these places will usually cater especially for a party, and some even sort out the cake! Ask when you book. There are other places to take slightly older children, like museums, zoos, theme parks; some gyms even have facilities for children's parties. If the children are older, you could consider the cinema, swimming, bowling, roller or ice-skating and then a bite to eat. The cost will probably prohibit the numbers slightly so stress this fact to your child.

What about a video?

If you have played the games and eaten the food, a video can be a very good way of finishing off a party. It makes the kids sit down and calm down if they are getting over-excited and kills the last half hour if you have run out of activities and games! Don't get a feature-length film, as they won't have time to see all of it – try cartoons or short stories.

PUTTING UP DECORATIONS

Decorating a home helps everyone get in the mood, it feels like a party and everyone gets excited. You don't need to spend much. Some people are more artistic and create all kinds of decorations. Others aren't so confident, but there are lots of decorations that are very effective but easy to make.

Make a large poster welcoming the children to the party, keeping the words big. Put the Christmas tree lights outside if the weather is fine, or in the main room if you are entertaining indoors. Provided that they are not of a distinctly Christmas theme and unbreakable, use other Christmas decorations as well.

Ask for help, even if it's just to blow up loads of balloons! Tie them round the room and on the front door to show friends where the party is being held. They can also be used in the games and taken home at the end of the party. Rub balloons on a woolly jumper to create static and they will stick to the walls.

Buy a roll of crêpe paper and cut it into thinner strips. Stretch them across the room and hang them down walls. This is very effective, especially for a Hallowe'en party.

DECORATION IDEAS

★ String up the birthday cards to cover walls or stand them on shelves. Use to play a game later: can guests guess who sent which one and can they remember which one is theirs?

★ Make mobiles by cutting simple shapes from coloured card or pictures from magazines and suspend them with cotton from a wire coat hanger.

★ Stick a bare branch in Oasis in a vase after spraying gold or silver. Decorate by hanging baubles on it, tying ribbons on the ends of the branches and even small biscuits.

★ Cut out your child's name from card and after colouring or spraying the card, hang the letters on a string across the room.

★ Fold squares or circles of white or coloured card into four and then cut out small pieces. Unfold them to make snowflakes to hang around the house or stick on windows.

MAKING PAPER SNAKES

Cut circles of paper round and round in ever smaller circles till you reach the middle. Hang them from the ceiling to make long 'snakes' that spin round.

Figure 1

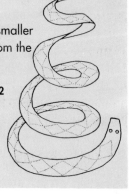

Figure 2

FORTUNE-TELLER

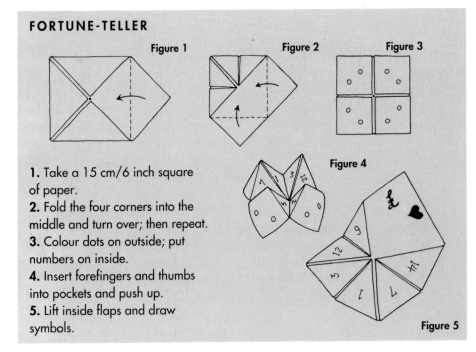

Figure 1   Figure 2   Figure 3

Figure 4

Figure 5

1. Take a 15 cm/6 inch square of paper.
2. Fold the four corners into the middle and turn over; then repeat.
3. Colour dots on outside; put numbers on inside.
4. Insert forefingers and thumbs into pockets and push up.
5. Lift inside flaps and draw symbols.

TABLE DECORATIONS

Cover your table with an old blanket to give as much protection from damage as possible. Use a plain white paper tablecloth, supply assorted coloured wax crayons and ask the children to decorate the cloth themselves. (Don't let the cloth hang down too far as it will get caught up and torn.)

Cut pictures of favourite pop stars and cartoon characters from comics and magazines and stick them all over the cloth. Draw speech bubbles coming out of their mouths and ask the children to write in what they think the characters would be saying. See who can recognize the most people: whoever guesses the most gets their tea first.

Supply pieces of card and crayons or pens, so the children can make their own place mats and take them home afterwards.

Use the cake as a table centrepiece. All too often the cake is only brought in when the candles are lit, they get blown out and the cake is whisked away and cut up for the guests. Leave it on the table so everyone can admire it, afterall it probably took you ages to make! Take it away from the table to

light the candles, though. It is too dangerous to lean across children using matches. You will also find they take great enjoyment in blowing them out as fast as you can light them!

If you don't put the cake in the middle of the table, tie a bunch of helium-filled balloons together and anchor them in the middle of the table with a heavy weight. Or tie one to the back of each chair, so the children can take them home with them at the end of the party.

Alternatively dress up favourite soft toys and sit them in a group in the centre of the table, so it looks as if they are handing out the food.

You could also fill a basket with small presents, balloons and sweets and put it in the centre of the table. The children can choose something from it to take home.

DECORATING YOUR GUESTS

Cut card into 5 cm (2 inch) strips and staple the ends of each strip together to fit round a child's head. Have coloured card, magazines and foil ready, to cut out feathers, leaves or geometric shapes. Colour them in and staple them to the headband.

TO MAKE PLACE NAMES

★ Write each child's name on a folded piece of card and put it where they are going to sit. Try muddling up the letters to make it more difficult!

★ Wrap a few sweets in a twist of crêpe paper. Tuck the sweets inside half a cardboard tube you have saved, and wrap up in more crêpe paper to resemble a cracker. Write the children's names on the outside.

★ Make small cakes and pipe a name on each with icing.

★ Write each child's name on a plastic cup with a permanent marker so it can be washed up and taken home. Or write the name round the edge of the plastic plate they are going to use.

★ Cut each child's initials out of stiff, coloured card and arrange them round the table. They have to work out who is sitting where.

FROGS IN THE POND

Make frogs from paper as shown.
1. Fold a square of paper into four, crease, unfold.
2. Fold corners into middle.
3. Fold two opposite side points into the centre fold.
4. Fold the smaller triangle at the bottom up towards the top.
5. Fold each new lower corner into the centre fold.
6. Fold up the bottom rectangle in half.
7. Fold top half of rectangle back down.
Fold the point of the top triangle down to make the head.
8. Turn over. Draw on eyes.
Press your thumb on the back of the frog, let it slip off and the frog will jump. Put a shallow bowl on the floor and see who can get most frogs in the pond.

Alternatively, cut wider strips and staple the ends together. The tops can be cut into shapes and the sides decorated with coloured paper, foil or tissue to make beautiful crowns.

Or ask everyone to bring a hat with them and to act out the character of the person who would wear that hat throughout the meal.

Toss small pasta tubes – macaroni or penne – in food colouring, spread out and leave to dry. Mix with cut lengths of coloured straws and supply lengths of string. Ask each child to thread themselves a necklace to wear for the party.

Write names of famous characters on slips of paper, such as 'Ugly Sister' 'Dracula' or 'Mr Spock'. Ask each child to pick a name out of the hat and then to use face paints to make themselves look like that person.

Thread colourful scrunched-up tissue paper onto a length of string and welcome each guest with a Hawaiian-style lei.

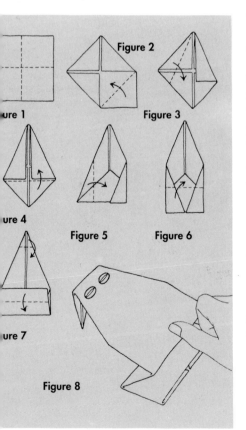

Figure 1
Figure 2
Figure 3
Figure 4
Figure 5
Figure 6
Figure 7
Figure 8

FUN AND GAMES

Games are an essential part of a party, children really look forward to them. They love games they know well and never seem to tire of musical statues. You will have to consider how much space you have as that will restrict the games you can play. Always plan plenty of games because they never last as long as you think, and some may not work as well as you hoped. Although there are games in this book specific to each party, here are some more games that you can plan ahead.

GAMES USING PAPER

PIN THE NOSE ON A POP STAR

Find a poster of your child's favourite pop star or cartoon character and fix it to the wall. Draw a nose shape on a

Games can be updated for older children, so 'Pin the Nose on a Pop Star', rather than the Tail on a Donkey, is ideal.

piece of card and cut it out; apply a piece of Plasticine to the back. Blindfold each guest in turn and ask them to pin the nose in the right place. They are not allowed to feel the edge of the poster and you may have to turn it round at different angles to keep them guessing!

ABOVE AND BELOW

Draw simple objects viewed from above or below on pieces of paper, pass them round the children and ask them to guess what they are. Play in teams or singly, the one who gets the most right is the winner.

PORTRAIT DRAWING

Have a large sheet of paper and some felt-tip pens ready on a table. Blindfold one of the children and lead

Animal Pairs is a good game to get the children talking and laughing, as they try to find out what animal they are.

them to the table, saying you want them to draw a picture of someone at the party. He or she must pick up a pen and has to draw the face, then put that pen down and pick up another to draw the nose, and so on until the picture is finished.

LADYBIRD, LADYBIRD

Give children a paper and pencil each, and a dice. They must take it in turns to throw the dice. They have to throw a six first to draw the ladybird's body. When a five is thrown, the head can be drawn; a four means draw one of the six legs; a three must be thrown for each eye; two for the feelers and one for each of the four spots. The first complete ladybird wins.

THE DRAWING GAME

Make a list of objects, animals, people and feelings. The children will be split into teams and one person from each team will come up to you for something to draw. You must whisper the same thing to each and they must

draw it for the rest of their team without speaking. As soon as the team guess it right another person will be up for the next thing to draw. The first team to finish the list wins the game.

MOSAIC MARVELS

Cut up lots of bits of coloured paper from magazines and comics. Supply paper, pencil, glue and brush for the guests. Ask them to draw a picture and then colour it in by sticking the coloured pieces of paper on it like a mosaic. Don't have a very large piece of paper or very small pieces of mosaic or it will take too long and they will get bored.

MUSICAL MATS

Save a newspaper and spread the pages over the floor. The children must dance around the room to music, stepping on the 'mats' as they come to them. When the music stops anyone who is standing on a 'mat' is out. Bring the 'mats' closer together as the children drop out.

SPACE FOR SPACE

During the week before the party start collecting sweet wrappers, yogurt pots,

cardboard tubes, cereal boxes, pieces of foil and anything else that could be used for building. Ask the children to work in teams to make a spaceship using anything from the pile of stuff you have collected.

ANIMAL PAIRS

Write the names of well-known animals on card in large letters. Cut each one in half. Divide the children into two teams and pin one half of the name onto each child's back. They must go round asking the others questions, like 'What colour am I?', 'Am I big or small?' The first two children to find their 'other half' are the winners.

BLINDFOLD ARTIST

Get pieces of paper, pencils and a blindfold ready. Blindfold each of the players in turn and ask them to draw something like a car. They can usually draw a simple object reasonably well by keeping track of what they are drawing, but when they have finished ask them to put on a roof rack, or aerial and then the game gets tricky!

THINKING GAMES

These games tax the brains and need concentration rather than creativity or action. Most are played sitting down and can be used at the end of a party to calm children down if they have become a bit over-excited.

EYEWITNESS

Take one child out of the room and dress him or her in an assortment of clothes – with a coat, hat, umbrella or newspaper to hold, and so on. Go into the room and give the other children a pencil and paper each. Tell them there has been a robbery and the police have seen someone running away. Call out POLICE! and the person outside must come running in, run round the room and run out again. The children must then write down a description of the robber. The one who gives the most accurate description wins.

TRAY CLEVER

Arrange a selection of things on a tray and ask everyone to have a careful look. Have fewer things for younger children, more for older ones. Take the tray away and remove one or two of the objects. Return the tray and ask them to say what is missing.

SAUSAGES AND MASH

Find a storybook and ask the children in turn to read aloud. Any words beginning with 's' must be swapped for sausages and any words beginning with 'm' must be said as mash.

LIMERICKS

This is a good game for slightly older children. Ask the first person in a line to say the first line of a limerick, for example: 'There was an old man of Peru.' The second child has to add the second line 'Who didn't know what to

do' and so on, until all five lines of the limerick are complete.

YES OR NO?

Everyone asks one of the players questions for one minute. The person being questioned must not answer yes or no, or they lose their turn.

I PACKED MY CASE

The first player says 'When I went on holiday I packed my case and in it I put a swimming costume.' The next player must repeat the sentence and add another item. Each player must remember the whole list before adding something else.

SLAP, SLAP, CLICK, CLICK

Get everyone to sit down and choose a leader. The leader must choose a category, such as colours or animals, and everyone must say the name of one in turn. At the same time they have to slap their knees twice then click their fingers twice – and this rhythm is kept going continuously

throughout the game. The name must be said while the fingers are clicking and be kept in the rhythm. Anyone who cannot think of something or misses their turn is out.

TELL ME A STORY

Give one of the children a list of words, such as button, onion, hairbrush and photograph. Give them 30 seconds to think, then they must tell a story mentioning all the items. See who can be the most imaginative.

CHINESE WHISPERS

Get everyone to sit next to each other. Ask someone at an end to whisper a sentence in their neighbour's ear. They in turn must pass the message on. The last person to receive it must say what he has heard. You'll be amazed how much the sentence will have changed.

A test for anyone's memory! Have more unusual items for older children and familiar things and fewer of them for younger children.

OUTSIDE GAMES

These games need plenty of space and should be played in a garden or park. Most of them are team games and require lots of energy so the children will be ready for their tea!

THE ROWING GAME

Split the children into teams of five. Each team has four 'rowers' and a 'cox'. The rowers line up with their back to the starting line and place their hands on each other's shoulders.

The 'cox', however, faces the right way and puts his hands on the shoulders of the rower facing him.

At the word 'Go!' they must set off down the course, with the 'cox' giving directions and trying to keep them all straight. The 'rowers' are not allowed to look round! The first team to make it to the finishing line is the winner.

LIMBO DANCING

You will need a long cane or broom handle for this game. One person holds either end of the stick quite high off the ground. Everyone else has to lean backwards and dance under it, without touching it and without using their hands. When everyone has had a go, the stick is lowered a bit and they start again. Each time the stick gets a little lower. Anyone who cannot make it is out and the person who can get under the lowest stick is the winner.

THREE-LEGGED RACE

Pair the children up and tie their ankles loosely together with a scarf. The pairs must race down the course

and the first couple to reach the finishing line is the winner. If the children are older, make the course a bit more difficult. Have a hoop they must both step through, for example, or a hat to put on.

WHEELBARROW RACE

Arrange the children in pairs. One child walks on his hands while the other holds his legs. The pairs must 'walk' as quickly as possible down the course, without falling. Provided the course is not too long, when they reach the end, make them walk backwards to the starting line again!

ANKLE-HOLDING RACE

The players stand behind the starting line, then they must bend over and grasp their ankles. When the starter shouts 'Go!' they must race to the other end of the course, without letting go of their ankles.

WADDLING RACE

Split the children into teams of four. They must line up behind each other in a full knees-bent position, holding the waist of the person in front of them. When the starter shouts 'Go!' they must all walk to the finishing line, without falling over and collapsing! They will soon find out that they have to work as a team or they will fall over all the time!

BALLOON RELAY

Split the children into teams of four and stand them at one end of the course. Give the first player a balloon and they must head it along the course, and back again – no hands allowed! When they get back the next player takes over and runs up the course and back. The first team with all four members home is the winner.

BOULES

If you have a set of Boules then play with that. If not, you will need a golf or squash ball and several tennis balls. The idea is to throw the small ball first, then everyone takes turns to throw two more balls as close to it as possible. Whoever's tennis ball is the closest is the winner and throws the small ball next time.

BALLOON SWEEPING

You will need five balloons and a broom for each team. The first player must sweep all the balloons down the course and back again. The second player takes over. The first team with

Older children adore tests of strength and Tug of War is a great outdoor game. Split the children into two teams to hold either end of the rope. Draw a line on the ground between them and the first team to pull the other over that line wins.

all four players, balloons and broom home is the winner.

BANG-BANG RACE

You will need a small paper bag for each player for this game. Split the children into teams and sit them in a line. The first player gets up, runs round the team and back to his place. Then he or she blows up the bag and bursts it. As soon as he or she has completed this the second player can start running. The winner is the team that finishes first.

BUN BOBBING

You will need a ring doughnut for each player suspended on the washing line by string. All players must put their hands behind their backs and try to eat a doughnut. The first person to successfully finish their doughnut is the winner.

THEME PARTIES

THE PERFECT PARTY GUIDE

* *

This section offers eight different theme parties that can be adapted for children of various ages. Each party includes ideas for decorating the house, invitations, and an activity for the children to take part in either at the party or before they come. You won't have to worry about the games as there are suggestions for each party.

PIRATE PARTY

● ●

Heave ho, me hearties! All kids like the thought of a pirate party, it sounds fun and you can certainly set the mood by sending out exciting invitations. Roughly tear sheets of greasproof paper and *carefully* scorch the edges on an electric ring or gas burner. Have a bowl of water to hand just in case! This is definitely a job for an adult but the kids can write the message and drop a blob of red food colouring on a corner for the blood! Leave to dry. Ask the guests to come dressed in scruffy, pirate-type clothes, jeans or shorts with a belt and a shirt.

If the sun is shining, organize the games in the garden if possible. Set the scene by turning the climbing frame or swing into the pirate ship, don't forget the skull and crossbones flag on the top! If you are indoors, rearrange the furniture for the boat, or just fly the flag from the front door and keep the room clear for the games.

When the children arrive, ask them to sign on board – scorch the edges of a larger sheet of greaseproof to make the ship's log. Issue them with a necktie, made from torn sheets or old fabric, and a patch to wear over one eye. If you feel very adventurous, get another adult to draw scars on the crew with face paints! Ask your helper to make, or have made, cardboard cutlasses ready for one of the games. Any adults helping must be dressed up, too!

FUN AND GAMES

PASS THE TREASURE CHEST

A variation on the traditional Pass the Parcel game! Instead of wrapping the prize in layers of paper, collect lots of different-sized boxes over the days before the party. Put the prize in the smallest box before sticking down and

Dressing up always makes a party special. Find stripy T-shirts, old ripped jeans, belts, chains plus old jewellery for treasure. Bare feet are best, but sandals or boots are also suitable.

MAKING A PIRATE PATCH
★ Cut pieces of black card to the right shape, large enough to cover an eye.
★ Make a small hole in each corner and thread thin elastic through.
★ Tie ends so it can be put on straight over the head.
Or thread string through, leave ends undone and tie round each child's head when in place.

Cut cutlass shapes from thick cardboard and cover with foil. Decorate with brightly coloured paper shapes or beads.

anyone the captain catches moving must go back to the start. The first person who gets close enough to touch him or her on the shoulder becomes the next captain.

BAGS OF FUN

Fill a black dustbin bag with all sorts of odd clothes, shoes, hats and so on. Place it in the middle of the room. Get the children to pass an orange round the room to music. When the music stops, the person holding the orange must, without looking, pull something out of the bag and put it on, no matter what it is! (Include things like leotards or false noses.) Start the music again and carry on until the bag is empty, but don't forget to have a camera handy!

JUMP THE RIVER

Put two pieces of rope or cane side by side but about 2 metres (6 feet) apart. While the music plays the children must run or jump from one side to the other. When the music stops all the children caught in the 'river' are out.

putting into a slightly larger box. Keep going, using a larger box each time. Put a little gift or sweet in each layer. Sit the players in a circle, start the music and pass the 'treasure chest' round. When the music stops, the person holding the box takes off one layer. Start the music again and pass the box on. Keep going until the winner opens the smallest box and gets the prize. If you are in charge of the music, try to make sure everyone gets a turn and wins a small gift.

MUSICAL CUTLASSES

Ask everyone to stand in a circle. Put all the cutlasses in the centre and take one away. Start the music and ask the children to walk or run round in their circle. When the music stops the children must grab a cutlass. There will be someone left without one and he or she is out of the game. Remove another cutlass and start the music again. Each time there should be one less cutlass than children so you end up with two children running round one cutlass. The one who grabs it is the winner!

CAPTAIN'S FOOTSTEPS

Ask one of the children to stand facing the wall and put all the others at the opposite end of the room. They must creep up on the captain, but he or she can turn round at any time, and

PIRATE PARTY FOOD

PIRATE GALLEON CAKE

175 g (6 oz) soft margarine
175 g (6 oz) caster sugar
3 eggs, beaten
175 g (6 oz) self-raising flour
1 tablespoon cocoa
2 tablespoons hot water
Butter icing:
175 g (6 oz) soft margarine
375 g (12 oz) icing sugar, sifted
1 tablespoon milk
1 tablespoon coffee essence
To assemble and decorate:
25 cm (10 inch) square cake board
6-8 ice-cream wafers
1 sheet rice paper
3 drinking straws
50 g (2 oz) brown glacé icing
1 sweet cigarette
red food colouring
1 liquorice allsort
8 liquorice comfits
2 Polo mints

Grease and line a 20 x 30 cm (8 x 12 inch) Swiss roll tin. Cream the margarine and sugar together in a bowl until light and fluffy. Gradually add eggs, beating well after each addition. Sift the flour and fold in with cocoa and water. Turn the cake mixture into the Swiss roll tin and place in a preheated oven, 180°C, 350°F, Gas 4 for 20-25 minutes.

Allow the cake to cool slightly before turning onto a wire rack.

Beat together the butter icing ingredients until light and fluffy. Reserve 2 tablespoons. Cut the cake into three equal pieces and cut one piece in half again (see figure 1). Sandwich the two larger pieces together with the butter icing.

Cut to shape and use two pieces

PIRATE GALLEON CAKE

Figure 1

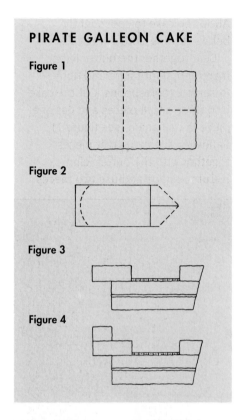

Figure 2

Figure 3

Figure 4

cut from bow end together to make a triangle (see figure 2). Cover cake and bow piece with butter icing. Place cake on board and position bow piece on bow.

Place two of the wafers behind the bow for the decking. Cover one of the remaining pieces of cake with icing and place on stern for first deck (see figure 3).

Halve the other piece, cover one half with icing and place on top and to the rear of the first deck (see figure 4), discard the other half. Place wafers on each deck at the stern.

Cut sails from rice paper and thread onto straws. Use glacé icing to pipe skull and crossbones on one sail. Press masts and sails in position, securing front sail with the sweet cigarette. Cut remaining wafers into strips and position as railings, ledges and windows all round the ship, and

press one into the side to make the plank.

Colour the reserved butter icing red. Decorate the ship with piped red dots and piped brown scrolls. Cut an anchor from the liquorice allsort.

Cut comfits in half and press rounded ends into the icing along the sides for the cannons. Position Polos and comfits as guns at the stern.

SAUSAGE CHAINS

Makes about 48
750 g (1½ lb) pork or beef chipolatas, linked

Leave sausages linked together and twist each one in half again. Pierce skins and place in a roasting tin in a preheated oven at 200°C, 400°F, Gas 6 for 30 minutes, turning carefully halfway through cooking time. Drain

on kitchen paper before transferring to serving plate. Supply kitchen scissors so the kids can cut off a sausage as they want.

GOLDEN NUGGETS

Makes 24
250 g (8 oz) plain flour
pinch of salt
2 eggs, separated
300 ml (½ pint) milk
375 g (12 oz) frozen sweetcorn, cooked
oil for deep frying

Sift flour and salt into a bowl, make a well in the centre and add egg yolks. Mix together gently with half the milk to make a smooth paste. Beat in the rest of the milk. Just before cooking add sweetcorn to the batter. Whisk the egg whites until stiff but not dry and fold carefully into the batter. Heat the

oil in a deep frying pan to 180°C, 350°F. Fry a few spoonfuls of the mixture at a time for 3-4 minutes, turning once, until crisp and brown. Drain on kitchen paper. Reheat if necessary, uncovered, in a preheated oven at 180°C, 350°F, Gas 4 for 10-15 minutes before serving.

'MOULDY BREAD'

Serves 12
large French bread stick
250 g (8 oz) crunchy peanut butter

Cut French bread stick in half if necessary to fit in your oven, but cut it diagonally. Slice diagonally almost right through the bread every 2 cm (1 inch) or so. Spread the inside of each slit thickly with peanut butter. Put the two halves side by side on a baking tray and place in a preheated oven at 190°C, 375°F, Gas 5 for about 20 minutes until crisp and brown. Use kitchen scissors to separate the slices and serve warm.

SHIP'S BISCUITS

Makes 36
175 g (6 oz) soft margarine
175 g (6 oz) caster sugar
1 egg, beaten
few drops vanilla essence
250 g (8 oz) self-raising flour
handful of cornflakes, crushed

Cream margarine and sugar in a bowl until light and fluffy. Beat in the egg, vanilla essence and flour to form a soft dough. Spread the cornflakes on a plate and roll spoonfuls of biscuit mixture in them. Place on greased baking sheet, leaving spaces between them. Flatten slightly and place in a

Sausage Chains, Golden Nuggets and Mouldy Bread are sure to be popular and the Ship's Biscuits and the tasty Cannonballs will disappear like a shot!

preheated oven at 180°C, 350°F, Gas 4 for 20 minutes or until pale golden brown. Allow to cool slightly before transferring to a wire rack to finish cooling. Eat while fresh otherwise the cornflakes lose their crispness.

CANNONBALLS

Makes 24
375 g (12 oz) chocolate cake crumbs
250 g (8 oz) chocolate and hazelnut
    spread
chocolate vermicelli to decorate

Using a fork, mash together cake crumbs and chocolate and hazelnut spread in a bowl. Roll tablespoonfuls of the mixture into smooth balls with your hands. Roll in chocolate vermicelli to coat and leave to set in a cool place.

PIRATE PUFFS

Makes about 30
Choux pastry:
50 g (2 oz) butter or margarine
150 ml (¼ pint) water
65 g (2½ oz) plain flour, sieved into
    a bowl
2 eggs, beaten
50 g (2 oz) Cheddar cheese, grated
½ teaspoon dried mustard powder
Filling:
25 g (1 oz) butter or margarine
25 g (1 oz) plain flour
175 ml (6 fl oz) milk
¼ teaspoon dried mustard powder
75 g (3 oz) Cheddar cheese, grated
2 tablespoons mayonnaise
1 tablespoon parsley, chopped
salt and pepper

Melt the butter or margarine in a saucepan, add water and bring to the boil. Add the flour all at once and beat until mixture leaves side of pan. Cool slightly, then add eggs one at a time, beating vigorously until smooth. Beat in the cheese and mustard. Place teaspoonfuls well apart on dampened baking sheets. Place in a preheated oven at 220°C, 425°F, Gas 7 for 10 minutes, then lower the heat to 190°C, 375°F, Gas 5 and cook for a further 20-25 minutes until crisp. Make a slit in the side of each puff to allow the steam to escape, and leave them to cool on a wire rack.

For the filling, melt the butter or margarine in a small saucepan, stir in the flour and gradually stir in the milk. Bring to the boil, stirring all the time until thickened. Stir in the mustard, cheese, mayonnaise, parsley, salt and pepper. Allow to cool. Spoon the cheese mixture into the puffs.

CARIBBEAN DIP

Makes 450 ml (¾ pint)
250 g (8 oz) cream cheese
4 tablespoons natural yogurt
75 g (3 oz) ham, diced finely
6 tablespoons crushed pineapple,
    drained
salt and pepper

Put cream cheese in a bowl and stir to soften, then gradually mix in the yogurt. Add ham, pineapple, salt and pepper. Mix well. Serve with vegetable crudités – cauliflower, carrots, peppers and celery cut into sticks.

STOWAWAY BUNNIES

Makes 12
125 g (4 oz) caster sugar
2 tablespoons cocoa powder
2 egg whites
12 scoops mint ice-cream
12 round chocolate mints, halved
36 chocolate drops

Mark twelve 7 cm (3 inch) circles on two sheets of baking parchment cut to fit two baking sheets. Sift sugar and cocoa powder together. Whisk egg whites until stiff and dry looking, then whisk in half the sugar mixture,

2 tablespoons at a time. Fold in the rest. Spoon chocolate meringue onto the circles and spread to the edges with a palette knife. Cook in a preheated oven at 110°C, 225°F, Gas ¼ for 2 hours. Cool on baking sheets. Put a scoop of mint ice-cream on each meringue base. Use chocolate mint halves for ears and the chocolate drops for eyes and nose. Serve immediately.

JELLY BOATS

Makes 16
4 large oranges
1 packet orange jelly
1 sheet rice paper
16 cocktail sticks

Cut oranges in half crossways, then squeeze to extract juice. Strain into a jug. Use a small spoon to scrape out the membrane and pith, taking care not to pierce the skin. Arrange shells close together in an upright position on a baking sheet.

Put jelly in a measuring jug and pour on 150 ml (¼ pint) of boiling water, and stir until dissolved. Add orange juice and make up to 450 ml (¾ pint) with water if necessary. Cool slightly. Pour into shells and chill until set. When firm cut in half with a sharp knife. Cut rice paper into triangles and spear with a cocktail stick. Arrange one on each boat as a sail.

BUCCANEER'S FIZZ

Makes 2 litres (3¾ pints)
1 litre (1¾ pints) fruit cocktail drink
1.2 litres (2 pints) lemonade

Mix fruit juice and lemonade in a large jug. Serve with straws.

Pirates like to nibble between games so Caribbean Dip and dippers will be perfect. Stowaway Bunnies and Jelly Boats make a cool interlude.

PIRATE'S DELIGHT

Makes 1.25 litres (2¼ pints)
900 ml (1½ pints) milk
1-2 tablespoons caster sugar
3 bananas, sliced

Whizz half the milk, sugar and bananas in a blender until smooth. Repeat with remaining ingredients. Serve with straws.

Children rush around, getting thirsty. Have plenty of drinks including Buccaneer's Fizz and Pirate's Delight.

WILD WEST PARTY

Checked shirts and jeans are just the thing for any well-dressed cowboy or cowgirl to be wearing to this party! If they have got the hat and boots as well, so much the better! Or children can be red Indians in loose trousers or dresses and moccasins, with a belt and bow and arrow. If the weather is fine, then throw a blanket over the washing line and peg the edges out to make a tent, and hold as much of the party as possible in the garden. If you are going to be indoors, make a tent from blankets and furniture.

There are lots of possibilities for the invitations: an arrow made from a stick, with a message wrapped around it; or supply your child or children with plain sheets of paper and ask them to draw a picture of a friend's face on each, then write 'WANTED' above it! Write details of the party, time and place below. Send the invitations to friends and ask them to bring them with them to the party. At the party pin the posters on a wall and see if everyone can guess who's who – a prize for the guest who gets most right!

The garden is obviously the best place for a Wild West Party, but an indoor hoe-down can be just as effective! Cut large cardboard boxes (usually available in big supermarkets) into cactus shapes and paint them bright green and, if possible, drape green fabric over the furniture to make the hills.

MAKING A SHERIFF'S BADGE

★ Cut out lots of sheriff badge shapes from card.
★ Ask the children to decorate one, or write their name on it to wear for the party.
★ Stick a safety pin on the back or use wide double-sided sticky tape.

MAKING A TOTEM POLE

★ Collect lots of boxes from the supermarket over the weeks before the party.
★ Supply the children with paints, crayons or gummed paper and ask them to decorate each side of the box to look like a face. (Do this in the garden if possible!)
★ Stack the boxes one on top of another to make the totem pole.

FUN AND GAMES

HANKY HURLING

This is a game only really strong people can play! Ask players to stand behind a marked line and take it in turns to see who can throw a handkerchief the furthest. Each throw must be measured and the longest throw wins!

KNOTS

Send one child out of the room. Ask the others to join hands and make a circle. They must then tie themselves in knots by stepping over arms, turning round, weaving themselves together but without letting go of hands. When they are ready, the other player must come in and untangle them, but without breaking the circle!

HUNT THE BILLYCAN

Ask one cowboy or cowgirl to leave the room. The others must hide a billycan or other small pan somewhere. The player comes back in and starts to look for the hidden object. Everyone must help by calling 'Colder, freezing!' the further away he or she gets, or 'Warmer, hot, boiling' the closer he or she gets to finding it. This is a good game to play in a garden as there are probably more hiding places.

ROLL 'EM COWBOYS!

You will need six pieces of card about 20 cm (8 inches) square. Round off the corners with scissors and draw one large dot on one, two dots on the next, then three and so on, so each one looks like the side of a dice. Make a hole in the centre of one edge of each square and tie 3 metres (10 feet) of string to it. Tie the other end to a pencil. Sit all the players in a line, pencils in hand, string unravelled and dice attached but over the other side of the room! On the word 'Go!' they

must twist the pencil so the string rolls up round it. The first one to wind up their dice completely is the winner.

STORY BOARD

This requires you to use your powers of imagination. Make up a story about the people in the room. Every time their name, or the character they have come as, is mentioned they must stand up, turn round and sit down again. Whenever you say the word 'posse' they must all do it together! Ask the children to do some of the story-telling too. Anyone who misses their cue has to perform a forfeit, such as singing a song, until their name is mentioned again.

Getting the kids to tie themselves in knots is guaranteed to cause much laughter and, possibly, a lot of falling over. Make sure you have a camera at hand to capture those amusing moments.

WILD WEST PARTY FOOD

BARBECUE CAKE

Try this moist dark chocolate cake instead of the usual Victoria sandwich.

275 g (9 oz) cocoa
875 ml (1½ pints) boiling water
500 g (1 lb) butter
975 g (2 lb) granulated sugar
675 g (1½ lb) plain flour
2 teaspoons bicarbonate of soda
1¼ teaspoons baking powder
8 eggs
Fondant icing:
3 egg whites
3 tablespoons liquid glucose
1.5 kg (3 lb) icing sugar
To assemble and decorate:
25 cm (10 inch) cake board
apricot jam
pink, brown, black, red and green
    food colourings
cornflour for dusting
dried spaghetti or satay sticks
cocktail sticks
foil
candles (optional)

Grease and line a 25 cm (10 inch) deep square cake tin.Mix cocoa and boiling water together until smooth. Leave to cool completely. Cream butter and sugar together in a large bowl until light and fluffy. Sieve the flour, bicarbonate of soda and baking powder into a clean bowl. Gradually beat the eggs into the buttercream, alternating them with spoonfuls of flour, and beating well after each addition. Gradually fold in remaining flour, alternating with the cocoa mixture. Mix thoroughly so an even colour is achieved throughout. Pour the cake mixture into the cake tin. Place in a preheated oven at 180°C, 350°F, Gas 4 for 3 hours, until a skewer

inserted into the centre of the cake comes out clean. Cool for 10 minutes in the tin before turning out onto a wire rack. Allow to cool completely.

Cut one third off the cake (see figure 1) and place the larger piece on the cake board. Trim the third of cake to the same length as the width of the cake on the board (see figure 2), and discard the smaller piece. Cut the larger piece in half again lengthways. Position on top of the cake (see figure 3, 4) using apricot jam to fix in place.

Put the egg whites and liquid glucose into a large bowl. Gradually beat in the icing sugar, using hands to knead together when the mixture gets too thick.

Colour two thirds of the icing with a mixture of pink and brown food colourings to give a brick colour. Wrap the remaining icing in a polybag.

Roll out the coloured icing on a surface lightly dusted with cornflour. With the help of a rolling pin, lift and drape over the cake. Use fingertips to mould icing so it covers the cake

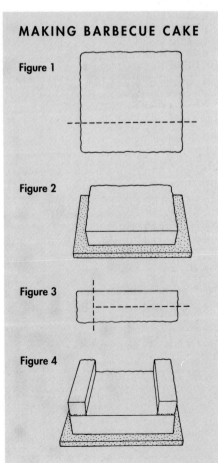

MAKING BARBECUE CAKE

Figure 1

Figure 2

Figure 3

Figure 4

completely. Trim off excess icing and mark the brick pattern with a knife.

Colour one third of the remaining white icing with the black food colouring. Knead lightly so that the colour is not completely mixed in and the coals will look hot. Roughly cut icing into pieces to resemble coals and arrange in the barbecue. Paint some with a little red food colouring.

Arrange double strands of spaghetti or satay sticks over the top and push into the cake to form the grill.

Roll out a small portion of the remaining white icing and cut into four circles, using a small cutter. Pile up to make a stack of plates.

Roll out the trimmings and cut out cutlery. Cut out small squares and fold into triangles to make the napkins.

Shape small balls of icing into sausages and burgers and paint with the brown food colouring. Cut out shapes and thread onto cocktail sticks to make kebabs. Colour 'meat' brown and 'peppers' red and green with the food colourings. Shape jacket potatoes and cut a cross through the top, as if for butter. Paint with food colouring and leave all to dry. Crumple tiny pieces of aluminium foil and wrap around the jacket potatoes.

Arrange all the food on the barbecue and add candles if you like.

PITTA POCKETS

Makes 12
1 kg (2 lb) sausages
6 pitta breads
sweet and sour sauce (recipe follows)

Barbecue or grill sausages until browned all over. Quickly run pitta breads under the tap and grill or toast for 2 minutes, until puffed up.

Cut in half and open out. Tuck sausages into pockets and top with sweet and sour sauce.

After all those games the kids will look forward to tucking into their tea. Pitta Pockets full of sausages and Sweet & Sour Sauce, Rustler's Ribs, Settler's Spuds and Salads should satisfy the appetite of the hungriest Cowboy, Cowgirl or Indian.

SWEET & SOUR SAUCE

Makes about 450 ml (¾ pint)
2 tablespoons oil
2 small onions, chopped finely
2 small carrots, chopped finely
225 g (7 oz) can pineapple pieces
6 tablespoons malt vinegar
1 tablespoon Worcestershire sauce
1 tablespoon soy sauce
5 tablespoons honey
1 tablespoon cornflour
salt and pepper

Heat oil and fry onions and carrots until soft. Strain pineapple juice into the pan and reserve pineapple pieces. Add vinegar, sauces and honey and simmer for 15 minutes, stirring occasionally. Blend cornflour with 6 tablespoons water and stir into sauce. Add pineapple pieces, salt and pepper. Bring to the boil and simmer until thickened.

RUSTLER'S RIBS

Serves 12
2 kg (4 lb) pork spare ribs
2 teaspoons soy sauce
2 teaspoons Worcestershire sauce
4 tablespoons tomato ketchup
2 tablespoons plum jam
2 teaspoons soft brown sugar
1 teaspoon mustard

Separate the ribs, if necessary. Mix all other ingredients together in a small bowl. Brush the ribs with the marinade and leave for 2-3 hours. Barbecue ribs until well browned, or roast in a preheated oven at 200°C, 400°F, Gas 6 for 1¼ hours until crisp and brown.

SWEETCORN SALAD

Serves 12
2 x 300 g (10 oz) cans sweetcorn
2 sticks celery, chopped finely
4 tomatoes, chopped finely
4 spring onions, sliced finely
4 tablespoons mayonnaise
1 tablespoon French mustard

Drain the water from the cans of sweetcorn and put into a serving bowl. Add the chopped vegetables. Mix the mayonnaise with the French mustard, spoon over the salad and toss thoroughly.

SETTLER'S SPUDS

Serves 12
12 baking potatoes
oil for brushing
salt
butter to serve

Brush potato skins with oil and sprinkle with salt. Slit each potato down the side. Cook in a preheated oven at 200°C, 400°F, Gas 6 for 45-60 minutes. If barbecuing, either put potatoes in the charcoal for the last 10 minutes or wrap them well in foil and cook for 45 minutes.

DEPUTY'S DRUMSTICKS

Serves 12

2 tablespoons honey
1 tablespoon Worcestershire sauce
grated rind and juice of ½ orange
1 tablespoon tomato purée
1 tablespoon soy sauce
12 chicken drumsticks

Mix all sauce ingredients together in a bowl. Brush sauce over chicken, cover and leave for at least 1 hour. Barbecue chicken for 15-20 minutes, turning frequently, or cook in a preheated oven at 200°C, 400°F, Gas 6 for 30-40 minutes until cooked and browned. Keep basting with the sauce to make the skin crispy.

CHOC CHIP COOKIES

Makes 12

125 g (4 oz) butter
50 g (2 oz) soft brown sugar
1 egg, beaten
250 g (8 oz) self-raising flour
175 g (6 oz) plain chocolate, chopped
   finely
50 g (2 oz) flaked almonds, chopped

Beat butter and sugar together until light and fluffy. Add egg and beat thoroughly. Mix in flour, chocolate and almonds.

   Place twelve spoonfuls of the mixture well apart on greased baking sheets and spread out to a 10 cm (4 inch) circle.

   Place in a preheated oven at 180°C, 350°F, Gas 4 for 15 minutes, until golden. Leave on baking sheets for 2 minutes before transferring to a wire rack to cool completely.

How can we finish off this party with a bang? Deputy's Drumsticks, followed by Choc Chip Cookies and Peanut Bars, with scrumptious Strawberry Milkshakes and Apple and Ginger Fizz to drink. That's HOW!

CHOCOLATE PEANUT BARS

Makes about 20
125 g (4 oz) plain chocolate, chopped
50 g (2 oz) crunchy peanut butter
4 tablespoons golden syrup
1 tablespoon water
75 g (3 oz) unsalted peanuts, chopped
125 g (4 oz) bran flakes

Grease and line an 18 x 28 cm (7 x 11 inch) baking tin. Put chocolate, peanut butter, syrup and water in a pan and heat gently until melted. Stir in the peanuts and bran flakes. Mix together thoroughly.

Turn into baking tin and level top. Chill in fridge until set. Cut into bars and serve.

STRAWBERRY MILKSHAKES

Makes about 1.5 litres (2½ pints)
375 g (12 oz) strawberries
2 tablespoons caster sugar
1 litre (1¾ pints) milk
4 scoops vanilla ice-cream

Place half the strawberries, sugar, milk and ice-cream in an electric blender or food processor and whizz until smooth. Repeat with the remaining ingredients. Serve with straws.

APPLE & GINGER FIZZ

Makes 1.75 litres (3 pints)
1.2 litres (2 pints) apple juice
600 ml (1 pint) ginger ale
ice cubes
1 red-skinned apple, sliced thinly

Put apple juice and ginger ale in a jug. Add ice cubes. Float apple slices on top.

CIRCUS PARTY

• •

What fun kids can have with this party theme! You could ask them all to come dressed up, or supply assorted funny clothes for them to use when they arrive. If it is a sunny day you could even have custard pie throwing in the garden, using crazy foam rather than the real thing. Decorate the house to look like a circus tent: cut sheets of newspaper or coloured paper into pointed shapes to look like bunting. Ask your children to make some posters showing some of their favourite attractions at the circus and put them on the walls.

To make the invitations, try cutting four small figures out of magazines and sticking them down on a piece of paper

(21 x 15 cm/8¼ x 6 inches) so they appear to be standing on each other's heads or shoulders. Draw a speech 'bubble' coming out of each mouth giving the details of the party. Make photocopies of this picture and send one to each guest – don't forget to include a tear-off strip so they can reply. Or cut out a seal shape from card and fold the base ends back so it will stand up. Write in your own party information. Ask the guests to send their replies on a picture they have drawn of their favourite circus act and give a small prize for each picture sent.

FUN AND GAMES

JIGSAW PIX

Tear large pictures of people, places or adverts from coloured magazines. Cut each one into pieces to make a jigsaw. Mix the pieces of the picture together and ask each child to reassemble it as quickly as possible. Keep the picture simpler and pieces bigger for younger children. Don't make them too difficult as they will soon get fed up if they cannot do it fairly quickly.

THROW THE SMILE

Ask the children to sit in a circle. They must all look very serious. One player, however, is allowed a smile. He

or she must run his hands down his face, wiping the smile off. He then 'throws' the smile to someone else, who can start smiling and trying to make the others laugh. The 'thrower', of course, should now have a serious face. The smile must be 'thrown' around the circle, and anyone who laughs or smiles when they aren't supposed to is out!

TIGHTROPE WALKING

Don't panic, I'm not suggesting the children walk along the washing line! Divide them into two teams and stand half of each team at either end of the room. Give one child from each team two bricks. These children have to race to the other end of the course using the bricks as stepping stones and moving them along. They must not step on the floor! If they do, they must start from the beginning again. At the other end another team member takes over and races back. Keep going until everyone has had a go – the first team to finish is the winner.

LADDERS

Ask the children to take their shoes off. Divide the children into two lines standing side by side. Ask them to sit down on the floor with their legs

outstretched and feet touching the feet of the person in the opposite line. Give each pair of children a number. Call out a number at random and that pair must stand up, run down the ladder, back up the outside to the top of the ladder and back over the legs to their places. The first one sitting back in his place is the winner and that team gets one point.

All clowns have to have a happy face for the Matchbox Game, but there'll be other clowning around anyway!

PASS THE MATCHBOX

You will need the sleeve part of a small matchbox for each team. Split the children into teams of six or more. Give the first one of each team the matchbox sleeve to put on their nose. They must then pass it to the nose of the next member of the team without using their hands at all, and they must pass it on again. The first team to pass it right down the line and back again is the winner.

WHAT'S THE TIME?

One child stands apart with his back to the others who gradually creep up on him, chanting 'What's the time, Mr Ringmaster?' The 'creepers' stand still as he turns round to face them saying 'It's 2 o'clock', or some other time. The Ringmaster turns back and the children start creeping again, still asking the time. When he calls 'Show time!' he rushes to catch them before they can run back to their base. Whoever he catches takes his place and the game starts again.

CIRCUS PARTY FOOD

CLOWN CAKE

250 g (8 oz) soft margarine
250 g (8 oz) caster sugar
250 g (8 oz) self-raising flour
4 eggs, beaten
1 teaspoon vanilla essence
75 g (3 oz) plain flour
25 g (1 oz) cocoa
Royal icing:
1 egg white
250 g (8 oz) icing sugar, sifted
To assemble and decorate:
30 cm (12 inch) square cake board
apricot jam
2 x 250 g (8 oz) packets of ready-to-roll icing
icing sugar for dusting
red food colouring
3 liquorice boot laces
red ping pong ball
liquorice allsorts
30 x 138 cm (12 x 54 inch) piece net thread
5 metres (5½ yards) gift ribbon
1 party hat or wrapping paper

Grease and base line a 20 cm (8 inch) deep round cake tin.

Sift the margarine, sugar and self-raising flour together in a large bowl. Add the beaten eggs and vanilla essence. Beat until smooth. Divide the mixture in half and stir 50 g (2 oz) of the plain flour into one half. Stir remaining 25 g (1 oz) of plain flour and the cocoa into the other half. Spoon mixtures alternately into the cake tin and level the top. Run a knife through the mixture to give a marbled effect. Place in a preheated oven at 160°C, 325°F, Gas 3 for 1 hour, or until a skewer inserted into the centre of the cake comes out clean. Turn out and cool on a wire rack.

Put the cake on the board, slightly off centre and brush the top and sides with jam. Knead the ready-to-roll icing on a surface lightly dusted with icing sugar. Roll out to a 30 cm (12 inch) circle. Lift the icing over a rolling pin and drape over the cake. Smooth the top and sides with icing sugar dusted fingertips. Trim off any excess icing, re-knead and colour it red.

Roll out and cut a red mouth. Dampen the underside with water and press onto the cake. Cut a length of liquorice bootlace and press onto the mouth. Add the red ping pong ball for the nose.

Beat together the egg white and the icing sugar to make the royal icing. Spoon into a paper piping bag fitted with a small plain tube. Stick two liquorice allsorts onto the cake with the icing to make the eyes. Pipe on an outline. Stick lengths of liquorice onto lines of icing. Stick liquorice crosses to eyes with icing.

Cut the net into three 10 x 138 cm (4 x 54 inch) lengths and put them on top of each other. Run a gathering stitch through the net (see figure 1) along one long edge. Pull gathers until frill is 30 cm (12 inches) long, and fasten off the end. Pipe lines of royal icing around the base of the cake (see figure 2). Press net firmly into the line of icing to secure.

For the hair, curl lengths of gift ribbon by pulling the ribbon over the blade of a pair of scissors (see figure 3). Stick onto the cake with icing. Trim party hat down to size or make a cone-shaped hat from wrapping paper. Make a bow tie from the trimmings. Add to the cake and complete with liquorice allsorts cheeks and buttons.

MAKING THE CLOWN CAKE

Figure 1

Figure 2

Figure 3

CLOWN FACE PIZZAS

Serves 10-12
375 g (12 oz) self-raising flour
2 teaspoons salt
75 g (3 oz) margarine, cut into
　small pieces
1 egg
150 ml (¼ pint) milk
Topping:
1 tablespoon oil
2 large onions, chopped finely
1 small green pepper, de-seeded
　and chopped finely
397 g (14 oz) can chopped
　tomatoes
2 tablespoons tomato purée
1 bayleaf
½ teaspoon paprika
salt and pepper
To garnish:
handful cooked peas
50 g (2 oz) mushrooms, sliced
6 slices salami
75 g (3 oz) Cheddar cheese,
　grated

If you prefer, let the children decorate their own pizza with toppings and see if they can make the face match their own!

Sift flour and salt into a bowl, add margarine and rub in with fingertips until mixture resembles fine breadcrumbs. Beat egg and milk together and gradually add to the mixture to make a soft dough. Turn out onto a floured surface and knead lightly until smooth.

Grease a 33 x 23 cm (14 x 10 inch) shallow baking tin and roll out the dough to fit.

For the topping, heat the oil in a saucepan and fry the onions until clear. Add the green pepper, tomatoes, tomato purée, bayleaf, paprika, salt and pepper. Simmer for 20 minutes until reduced by half. Work the mixture through a sieve or blend in a food processor until smooth; spread over dough. Cook in a preheated oven at 200°C, 400°F, Gas 6 for about 30 minutes until the dough has risen.

Cut into ten or twelve squares and use peas, mushrooms, salami and cheese to decorate. Return to the oven for 5-10 minutes to allow cheese to melt before serving.

SAUSAGE CATERPILLAR

Serves 12-14
1 large cucumber
2 glacé cherries
cocktail sticks
500 g (1 lb) cocktail sausages
6 rashers streaky bacon, rindless
　and halved
227 g (8 oz) can pineapple pieces
198 g (7 oz) can mandarin oranges
125 g (4 oz) mild cheese, cubed

Trim end of cucumber, use glacé cherries on halved cocktail sticks to make the eyes. Grill or fry sausages until browned. Wrap each halved bacon rasher round a pineapple cube and secure with a cocktail stick. Grill for about 3 minutes, until bacon is crisp. Drain on kitchen paper with sausages. Spear sausages with more cocktail sticks and arrange down the centre of the cucumber. Put bacon and pineapple rolls on either side with the mandarin oranges and cheese cubes in between.

ANIMAL CRISPS

Makes about 24
6 large thin slices of brown bread
softened butter for spreading
Marmite or meat paste, for spreading
2 small packets potato crisps

Cut crusts off the bread and discard. Flatten the bread slightly with a rolling pin. Spread with butter and the Marmite or meat paste. Crush the potato crisps finely and press into the spread side of each slice.

Use small animal cutters to cut out shapes – you should be able to get four from each slice.

ORANGE BANANA FLOATS

Makes about 1.5 litres (2½ pints)
5 bananas, peeled
2 tablespoons lemon juice
2 tablespoons clear honey
1.2 litres (2 pints) orange juice
6 scoops vanilla ice-cream
6 orange slices

Chop bananas and work through a sieve, beating in lemon juice and honey. Alternatively blend all together in a food processor until smooth. Add half the orange juice and blend again. Pour mixture into a large jug and add remaining juice. Put a scoop of ice-cream in the bottom of glasses and add juice to each. Decorate with orange slices before serving with spoons or thick straws.

TIGHTROPE WALKER'S WINGS

Makes 24
3 egg yolks
50 g (2 oz) caster sugar
120 ml (4 fl oz) single cream
2 teaspoons vanilla essence
275 g (9 oz) plain flour
oil for deep frying
icing sugar

Beat together egg yolks, caster sugar, cream and vanilla essence in a bowl. Add flour and mix to make a smooth dough. Roll out quite thinly on a lightly floured surface. Cut into 24 diamond shapes, using a wheel cutter.

Make a small cut in the centre of each diamond, tuck points through and pull out slightly.

Fill a pan one-third full of oil and heat to 190°C, 375°F, or until a cube of bread browns in 30 seconds. Lower pastry shapes into the hot oil, a few at a time. Deep fry for 3-4 minutes, or until golden brown. Drain on kitchen paper and dust with sifted icing sugar.

Red noses might have to be removed to drink a delicious Orange Banana Float! Serve with Animal Crisps and Tightrope Walker's Wings for the real circus flavour!

CHOC CARAMEL SQUARES

Makes 16
125 g (4 oz) butter or margarine
50 g (2 oz) caster sugar
125 g (4 oz) plain flour
50 g (2 oz) ground rice
Filling:
125 g (4 oz) butter or margarine
50 g (2 oz) caster sugar
2 tablespoons golden syrup
196 g (7 oz) can condensed milk
Topping:
125 g (4 oz) plain chocolate
2 tablespoons milk

Grease a shallow 20 cm (8 inch) square tin.

Cream the butter or margarine and sugar together until light and fluffy. Add the flour and rice and stir until the mixture binds together. Knead until smooth.

Roll out to a square and press evenly into tin. Prick well. Place in a preheated oven at 180°C, 350°F, Gas 4 for 30 minutes. Cool in the tin.

Put the filling ingredients in a pan and heat gently until the sugar dissolves. Bring slowly to the boil and then cook, stirring, for 5-7 minutes until golden. Spread over the base and leave to set.

For the topping, put the chocolate and milk in a small pan and heat *gently* until melted. Do not boil. Spread over the caramel filling and leave to set. Cut into 5 cm (2 inch) squares.

A favourite trick with clowns has always been staggering around with a bucket that the crowd thinks is full of water. But when he eventually throws the contents at someone they are showered with tiny pieces of paper! The birthday clown could try this trick on one of the guests!

CHOC FUDGE CAKES

Makes 15
125 g (4 oz) plain chocolate
300 ml (½ pint) milk
125 g (4 oz) soft brown sugar
125 g (4 oz) butter or margarine
125 g (4 oz) caster sugar
2 eggs, separated
250 g (8 oz) plain flour
1 teaspoon bicarbonate of soda
Butter icing:
25 g (1 oz) butter or margarine
1-2 tablespoons milk
125 g (4 oz) icing sugar
1 tablespoon cocoa powder

Grease and line an 18 x 28 cm (7 x 11 inch) baking tin, allowing the paper to come 2.5 cm (1 inch) above the tin on two opposite sides.

Put the chocolate, 4 tablespoons of the milk and brown sugar in a pan. Heat gently, stirring, until melted. Stir in the remaining milk.

Cream the butter or margarine and caster sugar until light and fluffy, then beat in eggs yolks.

Sift the flour and bicarbonate of soda together. Add the creamed mixture to the chocolate mixture and beat until smooth.

Whisk the egg whites until they form soft peaks. Fold 1 tablespoon of egg white into the mixture to lighten it, then carefully fold in the rest.

Turn into prepared tin and cook in a preheated oven at 180°C, 350°F, Gas 4 for 50 minutes, until the cake springs back when lightly pressed. Turn onto a wire rack to cool slightly.

To make the icing, put butter or margarine and 1 tablespoon of milk in a small pan and heat gently until melted. Sift the icing sugar and cocoa together and add to pan, mixing well until smooth. Add a little more milk if necessary. Pour over the warm cake and spread evenly to the edges. Allow to set completely before cutting the cake into squares.

FIRE EATER'S FIZZ

Makes 2 litres (3½ pints)
1.2 litres (2 pints) ginger beer
250 ml (8 fl oz) lemon squash
600 ml (1 pint) soda water
1 lemon, sliced thinly

Put ginger beer and lemon squash in a large jug. Top up with soda water and float lemon slices on the top.

It's a well-known fact that sticky chocolate cakes are a firm favourite with clowns, especially ones at parties! Anyone who is really thirsty will need Fire Eater's Fizz to quench the flames.

ADVENTURE PARTY

● ●

Have this party out of doors, if possible, as the theme is adventure and the outdoor life. Ask the children to come in shorts and T-shirts if it is warm and bring along any pith helmets and rucksacks! If it is a winter party, they could come prepared for trekking to the North or South Poles!

Make it an exciting and action-packed party – you could even take the kids to an adventure playground. There they can run around as much as they like and make their own games, so you will have less organizing to do. But it can be just as good at home!

Make an improvised tent for them to play in out of tables, chairs and blankets, or cover the lower half of bunk beds by hanging sheets round the edge. (Remember to remove all the bedding first, to prevent it getting spoiled by crumbs of food and spilt drinks.) The rest of the house will not need much decorating as the 'den' will be the focal point.

Draw a map on a postcard for the invitation, asking the children to follow the map, avoiding all hazards on the way. Or write the invitation details in code: use the code A=1, B=2 and so on to make it quite easy. The code must be 'cracked' or they will not know when or where to come!

Wrap the food in individual ration packs and give one to each child. If you are taking them out, ask the children to bring a rucksack to carry their food. All the food can be prepared on the morning of the party and wrapped in cling film or foil. (It also means there won't be a table to lay!) If you are having the party inside, spread a groundsheet or old blanket on the floor to give a real outdoor feel.

The children might like to work in teams to make their treasure maps as they can be quite time-consuming. The symbols can either be drawn or cut out, so have the right equipment ready.

MAKING TREASURE MAPS

If you have paper and pencils handy when the children arrive, set them to draw a treasure map each, putting in jungles, swamps and mountains! Here are some symbols to help them.

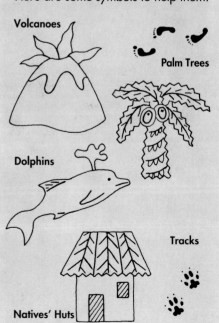

Volcanoes

Palm Trees

Dolphins

Tracks

Natives' Huts

FUN AND GAMES

EAT THE CHOCOLATE

Have a hat, scarf, large pair of gloves or gauntlets and a coat ready. You will also need a dice, a large bar of chocolate on an old plate, and a knife and fork. Get the children to sit in a circle with all these things in the centre. They must take turns throwing the dice. As soon as someone throws a six, he or she must leap up, put on all the clothes and start to eat the chocolate, using the knife and fork. Meanwhile the others are still throwing the dice. As soon as someone else throws a six, the first person must stop eating and take off all the awkward clothes for the next person to have a go! Sometimes the children don't even get a chance to put all the clothes on, let alone eat anything – so the game becomes a mad rush to get at the chocolate.

SPOONS AND STRING

You will need two wooden spoons and 2 metres (6 feet) of string. Tie a wooden spoon at either end of the string. Split the children into teams of four and stand each team in a line. The first person must pass one of the spoons down the front of their clothing and the next person must pass it back up theirs. But because of the length of string three people will possibly be linked together. The first team to get both spoons and all the string to the other end of their line wins.

THE POSTING GAME

Before the party, find eight jam jars and label each of them clearly with the name of a city anywhere in the world. Dot them around the house or garden, but don't make them too hard to spot. Cut up lots of scrap paper and write the name of each city on about

The Spoons and String Game is often called the Giggling Game and you'll soon find out why! Try having the string even longer.

25 pieces, (25 with New York, 25 with London and so on). Mix them together in a bag or bowl. When the game begins give each child a slip of paper at random. Ask them to write their name on the back and then go and find the right jam jar to post it in. They must then rush back for another one to post, the winner is the one who posts the most. Set a time limit and this will make them rush about even more, especially if you start a count down near the end: 'Two minutes!', 'Only 30 seconds left!' has them all out of breath and makes the game more exciting.

TOILET ROLL ROLLING

Split the children into two teams and ask them to stand in two lines facing the same direction. The first person is given a full toilet tissue roll and has to hold the loose end and pass the roll over his or her head to the person standing behind. They in turn must pass it back down the line over his or her head. The last person has the tricky task of taking the roll down through his or her legs and passing it back to the front through all the legs. The team must carry on doing this to unwind the whole roll in this way without it breaking. The team must then walk forward 10 metres (10 yards) to the winning line. The first team to cross the line, toilet roll intact and still standing wins.

WINK THE MURDERER

Tell the children to decide who will be the detective. This child has to leave the room. Ask the other children to sit round the room and decide who is going to be the murderer. Then the detective can come back in. He or she stands in the centre of the room. When the murderer winks at one of the others they must 'die', as theatrically as possible. The detective's job is to watch carefully, decide who is the murderer and point him out – hopefully, before the murderer is the only one left!

ADVENTURE PARTY FOOD

MIGHTY MOUNTAIN CAKE

19 cm (7 inch) sponge flan case
1 litre round tub rippled ice-cream
4 egg whites
125 g (4 oz) caster sugar

Put the flan case onto a flat ovenproof dish. Dip the tub of ice-cream briefly into hot water and turn it out into the flan case. Put this into the freezer.

Whisk the egg whites until stiff but not dry and whisk in the sugar a little at a time. Quickly spread the meringue over the ice-cream and pull it into peaks. Bake in a preheated oven at 230°C, 450°F, Gas 8 for 5 minutes until peaks are pale golden brown. Serve immediately.

The Mighty Mountain Cake can be covered in the meringue mixture, returned to the freezer and cooked later if preferred. It can also be cooked and frozen, although the meringue may go a little more rubbery.

PIONEER'S PASTIES

The filling can be changed to suit different tastes: use chicken or fish in a tasty white sauce, or spicy lentils for any vegetarians.

Makes 12

250 g (8 oz) streaky bacon
   rashers, rindless
1 medium onion, chopped
250 g (8 oz) minced beef
227 g (7½ oz) can baked beans in
   tomato sauce
1 teaspoon Worcestershire sauce
500 g (1 lb) shortcrust pastry
1 egg, beaten
2 tablespoons milk

Chop the bacon and heat in a saucepan. Cook until the fat runs out. Add the onion and cook together with the bacon until the onion turns a pale golden brown. Stir in the minced beef and cook for 10 minutes, stirring occasionally. Add the baked beans and Worcestershire sauce. Mix well and leave to cool.

Roll out the pastry and cut out twelve 15 cm (5 inch) circles. Divide the filling between the twelve circles, placing the mixture in the centre of each. Brush round the edges with a little beaten egg. Draw the edges up over the filling and pinch together firmly to seal.

Place the pasties on a baking tray and brush with remaining egg mixed with the milk.

Place in a preheated oven at 200°C, 400°F, Gas 6 for 25-30 minutes until crisp and golden.

Serve warm or cold.

MAD SCRAMBLES

Makes 12
6 tablespoons milk
25 g (1 oz) butter
10 eggs, beaten
125 g (4 oz) sliced ham or salami
½ cucumber, cut into matchsticks
salt and pepper
6 pitta breads

Heat the milk and butter in a non-stick frying pan. Add eggs and stir over a low heat until very lightly scrambled. Remove from heat. (The eggs will cook a little more in the heat of the pan.) Leave to cool. Cut ham or salami into thin strips and stir into the egg with the cucumber matchsticks. Season to taste. Cut the pitta breads in half crossways and open up each half to make a pocket. Spoon the filling inside

the pitta pockets and wrap in cling film to keep fresh until needed.

DAREDEVIL'S TEA BREAD

This is best made a week ahead and wrapped in foil, to allow it to moisten.

Makes about 12 slices

450 ml (¾ pint) strong hot tea
200 g (7 oz) soft brown sugar
375 g (12 oz) mixed dried fruit
300 g (10 oz) self-raising flour
1 teaspoon ground mixed spice
1 egg

Mix the tea, sugar and dried fruit together in a bowl. Cover and leave to soak overnight. Grease a 1 kg (2 lb) loaf tin and line the bottom with greaseproof paper. Add the flour, spice

and egg to the fruit mixture and mix well. Turn into the loaf tin and level the top. Place in a preheated oven at 180°C, 350°F, Gas 4 for about 1¾ hours. Turn out and cool completely on a wire rack. Serve plain or spread with butter.

MOUNTAINEER'S MINT BISCUITS

Makes 12

50 g (2 oz) butter
50 g (2 oz) caster sugar
125 g (4 oz) flour
175 g (6 oz) icing sugar
1-2 tablespoons water
½ teaspoon peppermint flavouring
175 g (6 oz) plain dessert chocolate

Grease an 18 x 28 cm (7 x 11 inch) Swiss roll tin. Beat butter and caster

sugar together until fluffy. Mix in the flour and knead to a smooth dough. Press into Swiss roll tin and prick all over with a fork. Place in a preheated oven at 180°C, 350°F, Gas 4 for 10-15 minutes until golden brown. Allow to cool. Sift the icing sugar into a bowl and mix with enough water to give a spreading consistency.

Add peppermint flavouring and spread over the biscuit base. Leave to set. Melt the chocolate in a bowl over a pan of hot, but not boiling, water. Spread the chocolate carefully over the peppermint icing and leave to cool. When set cut into bars.

All this food is suitable for packing up and taking out for a picnic tea. Just wrap the pasties, scrambles, tea bread and mint biscuits separately in foil or cling film and they are ready for transporting.

PEANUT POWER BITES

Makes 50
150 g (5 oz) butter or margarine
275 g (9 oz) plain flour
125 g (4 oz) cheese, grated
2 tablespoons water
1 egg, beaten
50 g (2 oz) salted peanuts, chopped

Rub the butter or margarine into the flour until the mixture resembles fine breadcrumbs. Stir in the cheese. Add water and knead with your fingers to make a firm dough. Knead lightly and roll out to a 25 cm (10 inch) square. Trim off rough edges and cut into five strips. Place on baking trays leaving space around them. Brush with the beaten egg and sprinkle with chopped peanuts. pressing them in lightly. Cut each strip into 5 cm (2 inch) squares and then in half to make triangles. Separate slightly. Place in a preheated oven, 180°C, 350°F, Gas 4 for about 20 minutes until pale golden. Transfer to a wire rack to cool.

POPCORNETS

Makes 12
8 tablespoons corn oil
125 g (4 oz) popping corn
4 tablespoons clear honey

Heat 2 tablespoons oil in a large heavy-based pan over a high heat. Add 25 g (1 oz) of the popping corn, cover and cook, shaking the pan constantly, until all the kernels have popped. Remove from the heat, pour over 1 tablespoon of honey and stir until evenly coated. Transfer to a bowl and repeat with remaining popcorn. Spoon into cornets or pockets and serve.

All explorers appreciate the extra energy they can get from peanut biscuits. They won't need a magnifying glass to search for the popcorn, cornets and toffee apples either!

CRUSOE'S CORNETS

Makes 14

3 egg yolks
150 g (5 oz) caster sugar
300 ml (½ pint) milk
1 tablespoon gelatine dissolved in
    3 tablespoons water
6 drops green food colouring
1 teaspoon peppermint flavouring
410 g (14.5 fl oz) can evaporated
    milk, chilled
14 cornets
7 chocolate flakes, halved

Put egg yolks and sugar in a heatproof bowl and beat until pale and creamy. Bring the milk almost to the boil and pour onto the egg mixture. Mix thoroughly. Place the bowl over a pan of boiling water and stir until thickened. Add gelatine and stir until dissolved. Strain and allow to cool before stirring in colouring and flavouring.

Whisk evaporated milk until thick and then whisk in the green custard mixture. Turn into a rigid freezerproof container, seal and freeze overnight. Transfer to fridge for 30 minutes to allow to soften a little before scooping into cornets and pushing half a flake into each one.

TOFFEE APPLES

Makes 12

12 wooden sticks or skewers
12 medium dessert apples
750 g (1½ lb) demerara sugar
75 g (3 oz) butter
2 teaspoons vinegar
175 ml (6 fl oz) water
2 tablespoons golden syrup

Push a stick or skewer firmly into the core of each apple.

Heat the remaining ingredients in a large heavy-based pan until the sugar dissolves. Bring to the boil and boil without stirring until 143°C, 290°F is

There is nothing like an adventure for working up an appetite – and nothing like the delicious discovery of Crusoe's Cornets, Toffee Apples and Popcornets at the end of the trail.

registered on a sugar thermometer, or until a little mixture dropped into cold water forms a hard ball. (Brush the sides of the pan with a brush dipped in cold water occasionally during boiling to prevent sugar crystals forming.)

Remove from heat and dip the pan immediately into cold water to stop further cooking. Tilt the pan slightly and dip the apples into the mixture one at a time. Lift them out, twirling them over the pan once or twice to make sure they are evenly coated with the toffee. Place on an oiled baking sheet until the toffee has set.

MAKING PAPER POCKETS

1. Cut twelve 30 cm (12 inch) square pieces of paper. Fold in half diagonally and crease firmly.
2. Turn the two creased points in to meet the third point.
3. Secure the join with sticky tape.

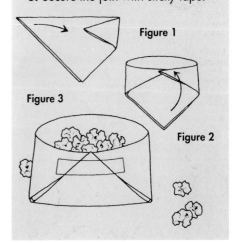

Figure 1

Figure 3

Figure 2

WITCHES AND WIZARDS' PARTY

This party could be a wonderful dressing-up party with costumes simply made from old sheets, black clothes, card and so on, and face paints used liberally! The children could make a hat or simple mask each at the start of the party. Close the curtains and keep the rooms dark. Hang streamers and pipe-cleaner spiders round the house, cut bats and other spooky shapes from card and dot them around.

The invitations will need to be spooky too! Write on black card with a silver or fluorescent pen, cut the card to the shape of a bat or black cat if you like. Or you could make up a spell and include the details of the party in it: 'Eye of toad, good and hearty, you'd better come to Joanne's party'…

FUN AND GAMES

APPLE BOBBING

Half fill a bowl with water and float apples on the top. In turn the children have to try to pick up an apple using only their teeth, keeping their hands behind their backs. If you are playing this game indoors, make sure you protect the floor and have towels handy. Or tie the apples on lengths of string and hang them from the washing line. The children must try to eat an apple without using their hands.

WITCHES AND WIZARDS

Each person will need paper and a pencil for this game. Get everyone to draw the face of a witch or wizard at the top of the page and fold the paper over so no one can see what they have drawn. They must, however, leave the lines of the neck showing, so the second person knows where to draw the figure to the waist. The third person draws the figure to the knees and the last person draws to the feet, each one folding the paper when they have finished. The paper must be passed on again for the fifth person to open.

MAKING A WITCH'S HAT

★ Take a piece of black card 65 cm (2 feet) square. Fix a length of string in one corner with a drawing pin. Stretch the string to the top corner, tie it onto a pencil and draw a quarter of a circle on the card. Cut out. Overlap the straight edges and stick down.

★ For the brim: stand the cone on a piece of card and draw round base. Draw a circle 2.5 cm (1 inch) inside the line and another circle 5 cm (2 inches) outside the line. Cut out central area and make small cuts every 1 cm (½ inch) from the innermost circle to the central line. Bend flaps upwards, place inside the cone shape and stick in place to make the brim.

★ Cut eyes from yellow felt.

WITCH'S SLIPPER

The children must all sit in a circle, with one person sitting blindfolded in the middle. Put a shoe or slipper behind the blindfolded person's back. You point to one of the children in the circle and they must stand up, tiptoe round the outside of the circle and back through their space, then up to the slipper and try and pick it up. Meanwhile the blindfolded person is listening hard and must point to where he or she thinks the moving person is. If he points correctly that

There's a ghost of a chance that your children will really enjoy dressing up in easy-to-make spooky costumes for this theme party and behaving like the little horrors they sometimes are!

Make hats and head-dresses by cutting thin card into shape and colouring with paint or pens. Ask older children to bring a hat they have made, or have shapes for them to finish off when they arrive.

person must sit down again and someone else has a go. But if the tiptoeing person manages to get the slipper, he or she sits in the middle.

WHO'S WHO?

Cut pieces of pop stars and famous people from magazines and newspapers, for example, hair, mouth and eyes, and stick them on a board or piece of card, all jumbled up. Put a number by each one. Give each child a pencil and a piece of paper with the numbers down the side and ask them to identify as many of the people as possible. The one who identifies the most is the winner.

FEATHERS IN THE AIR

Seat all the players in a large circle and stretch a sheet between them, to be held up to the chin at all times. Drop a feather in the middle. Each child must try to blow the feather off the sheet but not let it past them. They are not allowed to use their hands. If they are really good at this game, try adding an extra feather or two!

WITCHES AND WIZARDS' PARTY FOOD

GHOSTIE CAKE

500 g (1 lb) soft margarine
500 g (1 lb) caster sugar
8 eggs
500 g (1 lb) self-raising flour
Butter icing:
250 g (8 oz) soft margarine
250 g (8 oz) icing sugar
To assemble and decorate:
30 cm (12 inch) round cake board
6 x 250 g (8 oz) packets ready-to-roll icing
assorted coloured sweets
red, blue and black food colouring pastes
cornflour for dusting

Grease and line the bases of a 1.25 litre (2½ pint) soufflé dish, a 1 litre (2 pint) pudding basin and a 500 ml (1 pint) pudding basin. Beat margarine and sugar together until light and fluffy. Beat the eggs and gradually fold into the creamed mixture. Fold in the flour and divide the mixture between the soufflé dish and the basins. Smooth the surfaces and place in a preheated oven at 160°C, 325°F, Gas 3. Bake the cake in the small basin 40-45 minutes, the cake in the large basin for 1¼ -1½ hours and the cake in the soufflé dish for 1¼ hours, or until a skewer inserted in the centres comes out clean. Turn out the cakes and cool on a wire rack.

Beat together the butter icing ingredients. Cut each cake in half and sandwich together with some of the butter icing.

On the cake board, stack the cakes on top of one another (see figure 1), cut a slice from the front of the cakes. Cover cakes with remaining butter icing.

Colour 175 g (6 oz) of the ready-to-roll icing pink and use to shape the hands and feet. Leave to dry. Colour

MAKING THE GHOSTIE CAKE

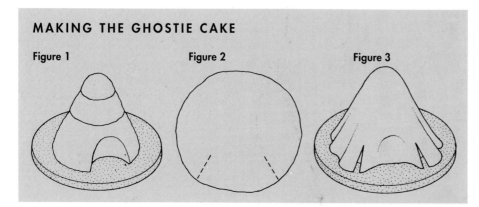

Figure 1   Figure 2   Figure 3

125 g (4 oz) of the icing blue. Dust with cornflour and roll into a 20 x 7.5 cm (8 x 3 inch) rectangle. Mould round the front of the cake to make a sweetie bag. Flute the top edge by pinching the icing and put hands and feet in place.

Roll out 1.2 kg (2¼ lb) of icing to a 56 cm (22 inch) circle and cut two slits in the front to allow the arms to fit (see figure 2). Drape icing over the cake, making folds to resemble a sheet (see figure 3). Using more of the white icing roll two 7.5 cm (3 inch) sausages and wrap them round the 'wrists' to make the cuffs.

Cut two small circles for the eye dots and colour the rest of the icing black. Cut two ovals for the eyes and two small crescent shapes for the eyebrows. Roll a long sausage and shape into the mouth. Fix all the features onto the face with a little water and fill the sweetie bag.

SPOOKY PIZZA

Serves 12
350 g (12 oz) packet bread mix
375 g (14 oz) can chopped tomatoes
2 tablespoons tomato ketchup
½ bunch spring onions, chopped
175 g (6 oz) sliced ham, chopped
227 g (7½ oz) can pineapple chunks, drained
150 g (5 oz) cheese, grated

Make up the bread mix according to packet instructions with hand hot water. Knead the dough on a lightly floured surface until smooth and soft.

Roll out to a 25 cm (10 inch) circle and place on a greased baking sheet or use to line a 25 cm (10 inch) pizza pan. Prick the base all over. Place in a preheated oven at 220°C, 425°F, Gas 7 for 10 minutes.

Meanwhile put the tomatoes and ketchup in a saucepan and simmer for 10 minutes until thick. Spread over the cooked pizza base.

Arrange onions, ham and pineapple on the top of the pizza. Scatter the grated cheese over and return to the oven for a further 10-15 minutes until

half. Thread a piece of orange, banana, a pineapple chunk and a marshmallow onto 24 bamboo skewers.

Spoon the chocolate dip into a serving bowl and drizzle two blobs of the reserved cream on top. Use a cocktail stick to draw the cream out into a bat shape.

TOMBSTONE SARNIES

Makes 12 sandwiches
1 thinly sliced high-grain loaf
50 g (2 oz) butter
8 tablespoons peanut butter
250 g (8 oz) cheese, grated
2 x 50 g (2 oz) punnets mustard cress

Cut the crusts off the bread, and using a plain round cutter or coffee cup as a guide, cut the top of each slice to resemble a tombstone.

Spread half the slices with butter and the other half with the peanut butter.

Scatter the grated cheese over the buttered slices and sandwich each with a peanut butter slice. Arrange the tombstone sandwiches on a plate and sprinkle cress around before serving.

bubbling and golden brown. Cut into slices and serve warm or cold.

BAT DIP WITH MALLOW STICKS

Makes 24
200 g (7 oz) plain chocolate
25 g (1 oz) butter
1 tablespoon golden syrup
6 tablespoons double cream
1 large orange, segmented
4 bananas, peeled and cut into
    large chunks
227 g (7½ oz) can pineapple chunks,
    drained
200 g (7 oz) bag marshmallows
24 bamboo skewers

Melt chocolate, butter, syrup and 5 tablespoons of the cream in a bowl over a pan of hot, but not boiling, water. Cut the orange segments in

These Tombstone Sandwiches aren't as gruesome as they sound!

STICKS & STONES SALAD

Serves at least 12

1 small red pepper
1 small green pepper
1 small orange pepper
½ cucumber
5 sticks celery
198 g (7 oz) can red kidney beans
198 g (7 oz) can sweetcorn niblets, drained
3 tablespoons parsley, chopped
3 fl oz (75 ml) sunflower oil
3 tablespoons white wine vinegar
½ teaspoon sugar
salt and pepper

De-seed the peppers. Cut all the vegetables into 5 cm (2 inch) strips and put in a bowl. Drain and rinse the beans and add to the bowl with the sweetcorn and parsley.

Whisk together the oil, vinegar, sugar, salt and pepper, pour over the salad and toss together.

ICKY CHICKEN BONES

Makes 12

12 chicken thighs
3 tablespoons soy sauce
3 tablespoons honey
2 tablespoons oil

Remove the skin from the chicken. Put remaining ingredients in a small saucepan and heat gently. Put the chicken in a roasting tin and brush with the warm glaze. Place in a pre-heated oven at 200°C, 400°F, Gas 6 for 30 minutes until golden brown, or the juices run clear when the thighs are pierced with a skewer.

Serve hot or cold.

WITCH'S BISCUITS

Makes about 20

250 g (8 oz) plain flour
175 g (6 oz) butter
50 g (2 oz) caster sugar
150 g (5 oz) icing sugar
25 g (1 oz) ready-to-roll icing
green, red and yellow food colourings
3 black and white liquorice allsorts
3 liquorice Catherine wheels

Sift the flour into a bowl and rub in the butter until the mixture resembles fine breadcrumbs. Stir in the caster sugar. Knead the mixture lightly to form a soft dough. Reserve one-third of the dough in a polybag.

Halve the remaining dough and roll out each half to a 20 cm (8 inch) circle. Put onto a greased baking sheet and mark each circle into six triangles. Chill for 15 minutes.

Roll out reserved dough and use cutters or card templates to cut out bat and star shapes. Put them onto a

Provide a spellbinding feast – Witch's Biscuits, Deadman's Fingers, Icky Chicken Bones, Sticks & Stones Salad and Brimstone Brew are sure to enchant.

DEADMAN'S FINGERS

Serves at least 12
250 g (8 oz) plain flour
125 g (4 oz) margarine
125 g (4 oz) cheese, grated
6 tablespoons milk
125 ml (¼ pint) tomato ketchup
salt and pepper

Sift the flour into a bowl. Rub in the margarine until the mixture resembles fine breadcrumbs. Season well and sprinkle in two-thirds of the cheese.

Make a well in the centre and stir in 5 tablespoons of the milk. Use your fingers to knead the mixture together to make a soft, but not sticky, dough. Knead lightly on a floured surface and roll out thinly. Brush the dough lightly with the remaining milk and sprinkle over the remaining cheese. Use a sharp knife and cut carefully into fingers about 1 cm (½ inch) wide.

Put onto a greased baking sheet and place in a preheated oven at 200°C, 400°F, Gas 6 for 10-12 minutes, until pale golden brown. Cool on a wire rack. Serve with tomato ketchup for dipping.

BRIMSTONE BREW

Makes 2 litres (3½ pints)
1 litre carton vanilla ice-cream
1 litre (1¾ pints) bottle lemonade
1 litre (1¾ pints) bottle cola

Cut the ice-cream into 24 small cubes. Put on a baking sheet and freeze until the ice-cream is hard.

Fill party cups two-thirds full with the fizzy drink of the chidren's choice and float two ice-cream cubes on the top of each.

greased baking sheet, spaced a little apart. Chill for 15 minutes.

Place the biscuits in a preheated oven at 190°C, 375°F, Gas 5 for 10 minutes for the small biscuits, and 15-20 minutes for the large circles. Cut the circles into the six triangles, as marked while they are still warm. Cool on a wire rack.

Sift the icing sugar and mix with enough water to make a thick paste. Colour all but 2 tablespoons green. Colour the ready-to-roll icing green. Make twelve 'noses' from the green

ready-to-roll fondant icing and reserve. Spread the bottom half of each triangular biscuit with green glacé icing and put the 'nose' in place. Cut the allsorts into four and fix on for eyes. Cut liquorice Catherine wheels into triangles and use to make the hats.

Colour 1 tablespoon of the reserved glacé icing red and the remainder yellow. Use a teaspoon to drizzle the red icing onto the biscuits for mouths and drizzle the yellow icing over the bat and star biscuits.

ANIMAL PARTY

If your child is an animal lover, then this party is a must for them! Decorate the house with pictures of animals, or ask children to draw a picture of their favourite and bring it along, giving a small prize to each child who brings one. If they have a small animal in a cage they could even bring it with them but be careful if you have pets yourself! If you want more of a zoo feel, then put paper bars at your windows and on the door frames.

Send out invitations made from pictures of animals cut out of magazines and stuck onto card. Draw a speech bubble coming out of each animal's mouth with the party details written inside. For more of a zoo approach, put a handful of monkey nuts in a small bag with the party information. Or cut card to the shape of a dog biscuit or lettuce leaf for a pet theme.

FUN AND GAMES

FLAP THE FISH

You will need to draw six pictures of fish, such as piranhas or sharks as well as more domestic types, about 20 cm (8 inches) long, on paper, not card. The kids could help you draw and colour them in with wax crayons. Six children at a time can play this game and they need to be sitting in a line with a fish in front of each of them and a rolled up newspaper in their hands. They must flap the paper behind the fish to make it move along. The first one to get his or her fish to the other end of the room and over the finishing line is the winner.

Finish off the frog costume using green gardening gloves.

PIN ON THE PARROT'S BEAK

You will need to draw a large picture of a parrot. Get the birthday child to help, but leave out the beak. Cut the beak out of card separately and put a piece of Plasticine on the back. Pin the parrot poster on a wall or board. Blindfold each child in turn, spin him round, give him the beak and ask him to pin it in the right place. The children are not allowed to feel for the edge of the paper. You can turn the picture up the wrong way or sideways sometimes to make it harder! The person who pins the beak closest to where it should be is the winner.

STROKE THE CAT

Ask all the children to sit round the room, preferably on chairs or sofas. One of the children must be the cat and crawl around the room, rubbing himself up against people and miaowing at them. The children must stroke the cat if it comes up to them but they are not allowed to laugh! Anyone who laughs is out. Let the children take turns to be the cat.

SLEEPING LIONS

What a fabulous game this is, especially at the end of a hectic party! The children must all lie on the floor and pretend to be sleeping lions. No one is allowed to talk, laugh or move. The child that remains still and quiet the longest is the winner.

WHAT AM I?

Before the party write names of animals on small pieces of sticky paper or labels. Stick one on each child's forehead without them seeing

MAKING AN ANIMAL MASK

★ When the children arrive at the party you could try this pre-arranged activity:

★ Let them cut out (or supply yourself) animal-head masks made from card that they can colour in or decorate.

★ If you don't have the time or don't want the mess then send the cut-out as the invitation and ask them to bring it back coloured in.

★ Make a hole on each side of the mask to knot string or elastic through to tie in place.

what you have written. They must find out what sort of animal they are by asking the other players questions. As long as the answers to their questions are 'yes' they can carry on asking more, but as soon as an answer is 'no', it's the next person's turn. The first person to discover what they are is the winner, but the others can carry on until everyone has found out what type of animal they are. Give older children harder animal, bird or even dinosaur names, but keep it quite simple for the younger ones.

Get the children to help each other with the mask-making as two pairs of hands are better than one.

ANIMAL PARTY FOOD

TORTOISE CAKE

Use two 250 g (8 oz) packets of ready-to-roll icing instead of making the icing, if you prefer.

175 g (6 oz) soft margarine
175 g (6 oz) caster sugar
3 eggs, beaten
175 g (6 oz) self-raising flour
1½ teaspoons baking powder
1½ tablespoons cocoa powder
apricot jam for brushing
30 cm (12 inch) round cake board
Fondant icing:
1 egg white
50 g (2 oz) liquid glucose
550 g (1 lb 2 oz) icing sugar
green, blue, black, brown and yellow
    food colourings

Grease a 1.75-2 litre (3-3½ pint) oven-proof bowl. Put a disc of greaseproof paper in the bottom.

Cream the margarine and caster sugar together until light and fluffy. Add the eggs gradually, beating well after each addition. Sift together the flour, baking powder and cocoa and fold into the egg mixture. Put the mixture into the ovenproof bowl and place in a preheated oven at 160°C, 325°F, Gas 3 for 1-1¼ hours until well risen and firm to the touch. Leave for a few minutes in the bowl before turning out onto a wire rack to cool.

Transfer to a cake board and trim to a tortoise shape. Cut out a small 'V' at one end to fit the head into, and small 'V's round the edge for each of the four legs (see figure 1). Brush the cake with apricot jam.

Put the egg white and glucose in a bowl and gradually sift in 500 g (1 lb) of the icing sugar, beating well after each addition. Knead the icing until smooth. (Alternatively you can use

bought ready-to-roll icing.)

Take 125 g (4 oz) of the fondant or ready-to-roll icing and colour it a green-brown using a mixture of the colours suggested. Use one-third to model the head, making the neck end in a 'V' shape so it fits into place. Mark the eyes and mouth. Divide remaining green-brown fondant into four for the legs, put into place and mark the claws. Colour a little of the fondant yellow and green and make a dandelion, if desired.

Colour remaining fondant brown and roll out until large enough to cover the cake. Lift using a rolling pin

and drape over the cake. Mould gently round feet and head, and turn it up slightly where it touches the board. Use a fine knife to mark the divisions on the shell (see figure 2).

Mix the remaining 50 g (2 oz) of icing sugar with brown food colouring and a little water to make a thick icing. Fill a piping bag, fitted with a fine plain nozzle. Pipe the lines on the shell.

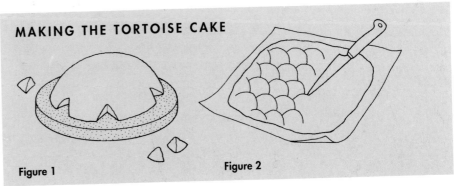

MAKING THE TORTOISE CAKE

Figure 1

Figure 2

Meanwhile, heat the oil in a deep-fat fryer to 190°C, 375°F, or until a bread cube browns in 40 seconds. Deep fry the chicken pieces for 12-15 minutes until golden brown and cooked through. Test to see if ready by inserting a skewer – the juices will run clear when the chicken is cooked. Drain on kitchen paper.

Deep fry the bananas for 3-4 minutes with the chicken. Serve warm.

Most children like takeaway foods so Southern Fried Chicken and Perfect Pizza will be popular choices.

PERFECT PET'S PIZZA

Serves 12

375 g (12 oz) packet white bread mix
125 g (4 oz) cheese, grated
2 tablespoons oil
1 onion, chopped finely
2 tablespoons tomato purée
2 teaspoons mixed Italian herbs
50 g (2 oz) mushrooms, sliced thinly
salt and pepper

Make up the pizza base according to the packet instructions and add 50 g (2 oz) of the grated cheese. Knead

SOUTHERN FRIED CHICKEN

Serves 4

4 pieces chicken, skinned
25 g (1 oz) plain flour, seasoned with salt and pepper
2 eggs
150 ml (¼ pint) milk
175-250 g (6-8 oz) breadcrumbs
2 bananas, peeled and halved lengthways
4 rashers streaky bacon, rindless
oil for deep frying

Pat the chicken pieces dry with kitchen paper. Dust the chicken with the seasoned flour. Beat the eggs with the milk in a shallow dish and dip the chicken pieces into the mixture. Coat the chicken evenly with the bread-crumbs. Coat the halved bananas in the same way.

Lay the bacon rashers on a board and run the back of a knife down the length of each one to stretch it. Cut each one in half lengthways and roll up. Secure with a cocktail stick. Place under a preheated moderate grill for 10-15 minutes until crisp. Drain on kitchen paper.

well. Roll out to a 23 cm (9 inch) circle and transfer to a greased baking sheet.

Heat the oil in a small saucepan and fry onion until soft. Stir in the tomato purée, herbs, salt and pepper. Cook for 2 minutes. Spread over the pizza base. Sprinkle the mushrooms over and top with remaining grated cheese. Place in a preheated oven at 220°C, 425°F, Gas 7 for 25-30 minutes until well risen.

White Mice and Chocolate Rocks are quite easy recipes so your children might like to help make them the day before the party. They can decorate the mice too!

WHITE MICE

Makes 12
2 egg whites
125 g (4 oz) caster sugar
24 split almonds
36 coloured silver balls
few red liquorice 'bootlaces' cut into
    10 cm (4 inch) lengths

Whisk the egg whites in a large bowl until stiff and dry looking. Whisk in the sugar a tablespoon at a time and continue whisking until very thick.

Spoon into a piping bag fitted with a 1 cm (½ inch) plain nozzle. Line a baking sheet with baking parchment and pipe the mixture into mounds, wide at one end and tapering off at the other. Neaten with a palette knife if necessary.

Place the almonds near the pointed end for ears and use the silver balls for eyes and noses. Place in a preheated oven at 110°C, 225°F, Gas ¼ for 2 hours. Cool on the baking sheets.

Make a small hole at the tail end of each mouse with a skewer and stick on a piece of liquorice to make a tail.

CHOCOLATE ROCKS

Makes about 15
25 g (1 oz) margarine
125 g (4 oz) plain chocolate
2 tablespoons clear honey
125 g (4 oz) bran flakes

Put the margarine, chocolate and honey, in a pan and stir gently over a low heat until melted.

Add bran flakes and mix thoroughly until thoroughly coated. Spoon into paper cases and leave to set.

CHEESY PEANUT BALLS

Makes 24
250 g (8 oz) full fat soft cheese
2 tablespoons peanut butter
75 g (3 oz) ham, chopped finely
3 tablespoons fresh brown breadcrumbs
125 g (4 oz) salted or dry roasted
    peanuts, crushed finely
24 cocktail sticks

Using a wooden spoon, soften the cheese and peanut butter in a bowl. Beat in the chopped ham and brown breadcrumbs. Form the mixture into 24 small balls. Roll each one in the crushed peanuts until evenly coated. Spike each one with a cocktail stick.

COCONUT FUNNY FACES

Makes 12
75 g (3 oz) soft margarine
75 g (3 oz) caster sugar
3 egg yolks
½ teaspoon vanilla essence
125 g (4 oz) plain flour, sifted
50 g (2 oz) rice flour, sifted
75 g (3 oz) desiccated coconut
6-8 tablespoons lemon curd for filling
To decorate:
4 tablespoons desiccated coconut
1 tablespoon cocoa powder
apricot jam
12 glacé cherries
12 small jelly sweets
angelica

Cream the margarine and sugar together until light and fluffy. Beat in the egg yolks and vanilla essence. Fold in the sifted flours and coconut and work into a smooth dough. Chill for 30 minutes.

   Roll out the biscuit dough very thinly and stamp out 24 circles using

Funny Faces are fun to decorate. Take care to remove the cocktail sticks from the Peanut Balls before serving to young children.

a 7.5 cm (3 inch) cutter. Transfer to greased baking sheets and place in a preheated oven at 180°C, 350°F, Gas 4 for 12-15 minutes until pale golden brown. Cool on a wire rack.

   Sandwich the biscuits together in pairs with the lemon curd. Mix the coconut with the cocoa. Spread a little apricot jam on the top edge of each biscuit and sprinkle with a little of the brown coconut, to look like hair. Halve the glacé cherries and fix two onto each biscuit with a little more jam to make the eyes. Add a jelly sweet for the nose and a mouth made from angelica.

FRUITY RABBIT

Serves 6 to 8
1 packet raspberry jelly
1 banana
50 g (2 oz) grapes, halved and pipped
50 g (2 oz) raspberries
750 ml (1¼ pint) rabbit mould
1 packet lime jelly

Make the raspberry jelly with 450 ml (¾ pint) boiling water or as directed on the packet, and allow to cool slightly. Slice the banana and add to the jelly

Jelly is a favourite so this rabbit will be a smash hit. Party Lights is a drink to cool down even the wildest animal!

with the grapes and raspberries. Pour into a 750 ml (1¼ pint) rabbit mould and leave to set. Make up a lime jelly in a bowl and leave to set. Dip the mould quickly into hot water and turn out on a serving plate. Chop up the lime jelly finely and arrange round the rabbit for the grass.

PARTY LIGHTS

Makes 1.2 litres (2 pints)
green food colouring
maraschino cherries
1.2 litres (2 pints) lemonade
yellow food colouring

Fill your ice-cube trays with water and then pour this water into a jug. Colour it green. Put a maraschino cherry in each compartment of the ice-cube tray and fill each one up with the green water. Freeze until solid.

   Mix the lemonade with the yellow food colouring to make it a bright colour. Put 2-3 ice-cubes in each glass and top up with lemonade.

TEDDY BEARS' PICNIC

A sk all the guests to bring their favourite teddy along to the party! Cut out teddy shapes to send as invitations. Ask your child or children to help colour them and write on the details of the party in speech bubbles. It is much easier to make one invitation and photocopy it than to draw individual ones!

If you have this party in the summer then it can be held in the garden, where it doesn't matter quite so much about the mess, but if you are having it indoors and are planning to let the children sit on the floor for a picnic, then make sure you cover the carpet. Spread out a large blanket or ground sheet for them all to sit on.

If it is indoors, buy a roll of cheap wallpaper lining paper from a DIY store and cut out and colour in trees and fences to put round the walls to give an outdoor atmosphere. Pack the food individually and ask each child to bring their lunchbox to put it in. There will be much less mess if you eat round a table, but if you do so put the food in baskets and add checked tablecloths to get the feel right.

MAKING A PARTY HAT FOR TEDDY

Before the guests sit down get them to make their teddy a party hat. Supply some tissue paper or thin card and sticky stars and shapes. Help the children cut out a crown shape to fit and then let them decorate them. If they enjoy the hat-making they could make a hat to match for themselves.

All children have a favourite soft toy, often a teddy, and will love the chance to take it to a party. They may even dress it up for the special occasion.

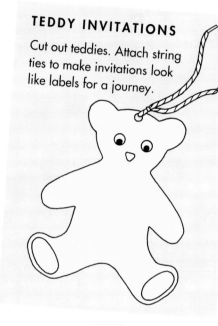

FUN AND GAMES

WHERE ARE MY SHOES?

You will need to get all the old plimsolls, trainers, wellington boots or other shoes out of the cupboard for this game. Ask the players to take off their shoes and then mix all the shoes together in a large pile in the middle of the room. The first child to find his or her own shoes and put them back on is the winner.

PASS THE BALLOON

You will need a balloon for each team, and a few spare. Don't blow them up too hard for younger children so they will be easier to pass. Split the children into two teams and stand them in two lines. The first person must put a balloon under their chin and pass it to the next person. The balloon must pass all the way down each line in this way without being dropped or touched with hands. If

calling 'warm' (close) or 'cold' (a long way off). This is also a great game for the garden.

ANIMAL GAME

Before the party begins, hide lots of sweets around the house. Split the children into teams of three or four.

Try to include the teddies in as many games as possible, especially as they are the special guests! Squeak Teddy Squeak and the Animal Game are hectic games but great fun for the kids!

Give each team the name of an animal – monkey, lion, cat and so on – and choose a leader. The teams must split up to search for the sweets, but only the leader can touch them. When another team member finds a sweet they must make their team's animal noise until their leader comes along to collect the sweet. Once the sweet is picked up by the leader, the team can search for more. The team that collects the most sweets wins and, of course, once they have been counted, the sweets can be eaten.

anyone drops it, the team must start again! The last person must start to pass the balloon back up the line between the knees! The first team to finish is the winner.

SQUEAK TEDDY SQUEAK

Ask all the children to sit round the room, preferably on chairs or sofas. Ask one of them to come into the centre and blindfold them. Give the chosen child a cushion to hold. Check that they cannot see and ask the other children to change places. Spin the blindfolded person round once or twice then let go. He or she must walk across the room until he finds someone, then put the cushion on that person's lap and say 'Squeak, teddy, squeak.' The child with the cushion must squeak and the blindfolded child must guess who it is. If he is correct, they swap places.

WHERE'S TED?

Ask someone to hand over their teddy and leave the room. The teddy must be hidden, then its owner asked back into the room. He or she has to find the teddy, but the others can help by

TEDDY BEARS' PICNIC FOOD

TEDDY BEARS' PICNIC CAKE

250 g (8 oz) soft margarine
250 g (8 oz) caster sugar
4 eggs, beaten
250 g (8 oz) self-raising flour
pink and green food colouring
18 cm (7 inch) square cake tin
Fondant icing:
2 egg whites
2 tablespoons liquid glucose
900 g (2 lb) icing sugar
To assemble and decorate:
cornflour
25 cm (10 inch) cake board,
apricot jam
green, pink, yellow and brown food
   colouring
candle
250 g (8 oz) white marzipan
doll's house plates, glasses and cutlery
thin straws
1.8 m (2 yards) thin ribbon
12 sugar flowers

Grease and line an 18 cm (7 inch) square cake tin. Cream the margarine and sugar together until light and fluffy. Gradually beat in the eggs and fold in the flour. Divide the mixture into three. Colour one third pink and one third green. Put alternate spoonfuls of the mixture in the cake tin, level the top and place in a preheated oven at 160°C, 325°F, Gas 3 for 1-1¼ hours until firm. Turn out and cool on a wire rack.

Put the 2 egg whites in a large bowl with the liquid glucose. Gradually add sifted icing sugar, kneading by hand when it gets too stiff to stir. Wrap tightly in a polybag.

Place the cake on the board and brush with apricot jam. Reserve one quarter of the icing and roll the rest out to a 28 cm (11 inch) square on a board lightly dusted with cornflour. Lift icing on a rolling pin and drape over the cake. Use hands dusted with cornflour to smooth icing into shape. Trim off excess. Re-roll and use to cover dampened edges of the board. Trim again.

Colour half the remaining icing pale green, roll out and cut a 15 cm (6 inch) square rug. Brush the top of the cake with water and position rug. Mark a fringe with a knife. Colour a little icing pink and shape a 5 cm (2 inch) tablecloth. Place in the centre of the rug. Mark 'embroidery' by pricking a pattern round the edge with a cocktail stick. Cut a small square of icing for the teddy bears' cake. Press a candle in the top, decorate side with a green icing frill and place a small strip of foil beneath it for a cake board. Place on the tablecloth.

To make the teddy bears, knead 250 g (8 oz) white marzipan and shape a piece into an oval 2.5 cm (1 inch) long to make the body. Shape the head, pinch the front to make the snout. Add two small ears. Shape limbs and press onto the body so that the teddy is seated. Mould more bears, varying their colours by using yellow and brown colourings.

Paint on bears' features with food colouring and allow to dry. Position the bears on the cake. Arrange the doll's house plates and cutlery around them. Pack pink and yellow icing into glasses to make desserts and drinks. Insert a short length of a thin straw into each glass.

To make the sandwiches, roll a small piece of yellow icing between two pieces of white icing and cut out sandwiches. Roll up thin pieces of brown and white icing and slice to make Swiss roll pieces. Cut two lengths of ribbon to fit around base of cake. Secure with a little icing. Tie a small bow and secure at one corner. Decorate main cake board with sugar flowers.

TAKE-OUT BURGERS

Hamburger buns might be too big for small children so use a smaller, softer bun for them.

Makes 12
12 beefburgers
12 hamburger buns
3-4 tablespoons mayonnaise
12 lettuce leaves
4-5 tablespoons hamburger relish
2 dill pickles, sliced

Grill the beefburgers for 2-3 minutes each side, until thoroughly cooked. Allow to cool.

Split the buns open and toast the cut sides under the grill. Spread the mayonnaise on the base of the bun. Place a lettuce leaf on top of the mayonnaise and then the beefburger.

Top with a spoonful of hamburger relish and a slice of dill pickle. Wrap the hamburgers in foil.

MINI-QUICHES

Makes 24
250 g (8 oz) shortcrust pastry
8 rashers streaky bacon, rindless
6 spring onions, chopped finely
175 g (6 oz) cheese, grated
3 eggs
300 ml (½ pint) milk
salt and pepper

Roll out the pastry, stamp out 24 circles with a 7.5 cm (3 inch) cutter and line bun tins with the pastry circles. Chop the bacon and fry in a non-stick pan until it begins to sizzle. Add the spring onions and fry together for 5 minutes. Divide the mixture between the pastry cases. Top each with a little grated cheese. Beat the eggs, milk and seasonings together in a bowl and pour into the pastry cases. Place in a preheated oven at 180°C, 350°F, Gas 4 for 20-25 minutes until set. Remove from bun tins and cool on a wire rack.

SUN'S OUT PIE

Serves 12
2 x 370 g (13 oz) packets frozen
   puff pastry, thawed
500 g (1 lb) sausagemeat
1 onion, chopped
250 g (8 oz) cheese, grated
25 g (1 oz) fresh breadcrumbs
2 eggs, beaten
6 eggs, hard-boiled
milk to glaze
salt and pepper

Carefully roll out each piece of pastry into a 35.5 x 25.5 cm (14 x 10 inch) rectangle. Place each rectangle on a dampened baking sheet.

Mix the sausagemeat, onion, cheese, breadcrumbs and beaten eggs together and season well. Spread a quarter of the mixture in a 5 cm (2 inch) wide strip along the centre of each pastry rectangle.

Halve the hard-boiled eggs, length-ways. Place end to end, cut side up, on top of the sausagemeat.

Carefully cover with the rest of the sausagemeat, packing it into a neat sausage shape. Damp the edges of the pastry and seal together. Turn each roll over, so the seams are underneath. Brush the pastry with milk and place in a preheated oven at 200°C, 400°F, Gas 6 for 40 minutes. Serve cold, cut into thick slices.

All the food included here is transportable if well wrapped, so try to have the picnic outside if possible. Pack it all into a basket and head for the woods!

CARROT CAKE

Serves 12
250 g (8 oz) self-raising flour
2 teaspoons baking powder
150 g (5 oz) soft brown sugar
50 g (2 oz) walnuts, chopped
250 g (8 oz) carrots, peeled and grated
2 small ripe bananas, mashed
2 eggs
150 ml (¼ pint) corn oil
Topping:
75 g (3 oz) cream cheese
75 g (3 oz) icing sugar

Grease and base line a deep 18 cm (7 inch) square cake tin. Sift the flour and baking powder into a large bowl and stir in the brown sugar and walnuts. Squeeze any excess moisture out of the grated carrots and add to the mixture with the bananas. Stir together. Lightly beat the eggs and oil, then gradually beat them into the mixture with a wooden spoon. Spoon the cake mixture into the tin and level the top. Place in a preheated oven at 180°C, 350°F, Gas 4 for about 1¼ hours, until a skewer inserted into the centre comes out clean. Turn the cake out and allow to cool on a wire rack.

For the topping, beat the cream cheese and sifted icing sugar together. Split the cake in half, spread the mixture over the base and sandwich together again.

FISHY BITES

Makes 24
212 g (7½ oz) packet boil-in-the-bag
    smoked haddock
25 g (1 oz) butter
25 g (1 oz) plain flour
150 ml (¼ pint) milk
2 eggs, hard-boiled
1 tablespoon parsley, chopped
370 g (13 oz) packet frozen puff
    pastry, thawed
1 egg, beaten
salt and pepper

Cook the haddock according to the
directions on the packet. Melt the
butter in a saucepan, add flour and
cook, stirring constantly for 1 minute.
Remove from heat and gradually add
the milk, beating well after each
addition. Bring to the boil, stirring,
and cook for 2 minutes. Flake the fish,
discarding all the bones and skin, and
chop the hard-boiled eggs. Add fish
and eggs to the sauce with the parsley
and seasonings. Roll the pastry out
thinly and stamp out circles with a
7.5 cm (3 inch) cutter. Put a small
spoonful of the fish mixture into the
centre of each circle. Brush the edges
with beaten egg and fold the sides of
the pastry in over the filling to shape
into a triangle. Pinch corners to seal
firmly. Arrange on a dampened baking
sheet and brush with beaten egg.
Place in a preheated oven at 200°C,
400°F, Gas 6 for about 20 minutes,
until crisp and golden.

HOT DOGS

Makes 12
12 frankfurter sausages
12 soft finger rolls
butter
tomato ketchup
3 tomatoes, quartered
12 small gherkins
cocktail sticks

Grill the frankfurters for about
5 minutes, turning them once or twice.
Split the rolls lengthways but do not
separate the two halves. Spread thinly
with butter and ketchup. Put a sausage
inside each. Spear a tomato quarter
and a gherkin with a cocktail stick and
serve with the hot dog.

CHEESY SCONES

Makes 12
250 g (8 oz) self-raising flour
¼ teaspoon salt
½ teaspoon dried mustard powder
25 g (1 oz) butter
125 g (4 oz) cheese, grated
150 ml (¼ pint) milk
150 g (5.3 oz) tube cheese spread with ham
1 punnet salad cress

Sift the flour, salt and mustard into a large bowl and rub in the butter. Add three-quarters of the cheese and enough milk to bind the mixture into a soft dough. Roll out on a lightly floured surface into a 20 x 15 cm (8 x 6 inch) rectangle and cut into twelve smaller rectangles. Arrange these on a greased baking sheet, brush with milk and sprinkle with the remaining cheese. Place in a pre-heated oven at 220°C, 425°F, Gas 7 for about 12 minutes, until well risen and golden. Cool on a wire rack. Split and spread the bottom half with the cheese spread. Garnish with a little cress and replace the top half.

SUNSHINE BUNS

Makes 12
75 g (3 oz) butter
1 egg, beaten
2 tablespoons milk
75 g (3 oz) caster sugar
125 g (4 oz) self-raising flour
12 paper cake cases
To decorate:
75 g (3 oz) butter
175 g (6 oz) icing sugar
lemon curd

There is something for everyone's tastes in the picnic hamper, from Fishy Bites and Hot Dogs, to Cheesy Scones and Sunshine Buns. All quite easy to make, wrap and transport.

Melt the butter in a saucepan. Remove from the heat and add the egg, milk and sugar. Mix well and then add the flour. Stand the paper cake cases on a baking sheet and divide the mixture between them. Place in a preheated oven at 180°C, 350°F, Gas 4 for 20-25 minutes, until firm to the touch. Cool, in the cases, on a wire rack. Beat the butter and sifted icing sugar together until soft and creamy. Put into a piping bag fitted with a small star nozzle. Pipe a circle round the edge of each cake. Fill the centres with a teaspoonful of lemon curd.

CHRISTMAS PARTY

There is so much going on at this time of year that Christmas birthdays can be overlooked. A birthday party ensures the day is special – and can be easy to organize: near Christmas the house will already be decorated and the tree will be up, so that saves a lot of work! Make sure you give out the invitations well in advance as there are lots of social events at this time of year and many people go away.

Try making biscuit invitations. Use special cutters for the biscuits and make a hole through the top before cooking. Thread a ribbon through the cooked and cooled biscuit and attach a card with the party details written on it. The guests can hang it on their tree or eat it.

Alternatively, cut Christmas tree shapes from card and ask your children to decorate them with sticky shapes and glitter.

It is also the pantomime time of year so you might like to ask the children to come along dressed as their favourite fairytale character. Send out invitations to the ball if you plan to have this theme!

Iced biscuits make festive invitations and are traditional tree decorations. Try Santas and snowmen as well as stars.

FUN AND GAMES

TREASURE HUNT

Gather together 12 smallish items such as a button, a crayon, clothes peg and so on and hide them round the house. For example, sew the button on a curtain, clip the clothes peg on a cushion – but remember to keep everything within the children's reach. Give each of the children a list of the hidden things and ask them to search for them, writing on their list where they saw each one, but not collecting them up. The person who correctly spots all the items is the winner.

SNOWFLAKES

Have plenty of pieces of paper ready folded into quarters. You will also need lots of pairs of scissors, crayons or felt-tip pens. Ask the children to cut

---

CHRISTMAS BISCUIT INVITATIONS

Makes about 15
125 g (4 oz) butter
50 g (2 oz) caster sugar
175 g (6 oz) plain flour
250 g (8 oz) icing sugar
silver balls to decorate
20 cm (8 inches) fine ribbon

★ Beat the butter until really soft, add caster sugar and finally the flour, a little at a time. Knead until smooth.
★ Roll out the dough on a floured surface and use a 6.5 cm (2½ inch) star cutter to cut out shapes. Make a

hole through one point with a skewer.
★ Place in a preheated oven at 150°C, 300°F, Gas 2 for about 25 minutes. Cool on a wire rack.
★ Mix the icing sugar with enough water to make a fairly stiff glacé icing and spread over the cold biscuits, taking care not to fill in the hole.
★ Arrange the silver balls at the points and leave to set. If you are feeling adventurous, colour a little glacé icing and pipe on the children's names.
★ Thread a length of fine ribbon through the hole.

patterns in the folded edges of the paper so when it is opened up they have a cut-out snowflake, which they can colour in and take home. Once they have mastered the technique, they will probably want to make more. Obviously this is quite a messy activity, so be prepared!

CHRISTMAS POST

You will need a flowerpot, a tray, lots of marbles and a fork for this game. Check that the marbles will fit through the hole in the base of the flowerpot. Stand it upside down on the tray surrounded by the marbles. Each child has one minute to use the fork to post as many marbles as they can through the hole! The one who gets the most wins.

SOCK FUMBLING

Take a large, thick woolly sock and put one item at the bottom of it without the children seeing it. Each child comes to you in turn to feel the sock and whisper to you what they think is inside. Have a mixture of items including some more unusual and puzzling things. When they have all had a turn, tip out the contents.

CHRISTMAS PICTURES

Before the party make a list of Christmas items such as reindeers, angels and stockings. Split the children into teams of five or six and give each team some paper and a pencil. Ask the first child from each team to come up to you, one at a time, and whisper to them the first item on your list. They must go back and draw it for their team. As soon as a team member guesses it correctly, the next member comes up for the second item.

Some children might like to dress up – as an angel from their Nativity Play, a fairy from the Christmas tree or someone from a favourite story book.

CHRISTMAS PARTY FOOD

THE NIGHT BEFORE CHRISTMAS CAKE

Assemble and decorate this cake a day ahead, as some of the decorations need to set overnight.

250 g (8 oz) butter or margarine
250 g (8 oz) soft dark brown
   sugar
5 eggs, beaten
350 g (12 oz) plain flour, sifted
1 tablespoon mixed spice
125 g (4 oz) glacé cherries,
   quartered
50 g (2 oz) mixed chopped nuts
125 g (4 oz) mixed chopped peel
300 g (10 oz) sultanas
300 g (10 oz) raisins
300 g (10 oz) currants
28 cm (11 inch) round cake board,
   covered with wrapping paper
Tree icing:
3 egg whites
3 tablespoons liquid glucose
1.5 kg (3 lb) icing sugar
green, yellow, red and black
   food colouring
Royal icing:
1 egg white
250 g (8 oz) icing sugar
To decorate:
silver and gold dragees
sugar-coated chocolate buttons
icing sugar for dusting
gold star
small wrapped sweets

Grease and base line a deep 15 cm (6 inch) round cake tin. Remove both ends from an empty deep 7.5 cm (3 inch) diameter can. Stand on a baking sheet and line in the same way.

   Beat the butter or margarine and dark brown sugar together until light and fluffy. Beat in the eggs a little at a time, adding a spoonful of flour if the mixture starts to curdle. Stir in the remaining flour and spice. Beat in the cherries, nuts, mixed peel and dried fruit. Divide mixture between the two tins. Place in a preheated oven at 140°C, 275°F, Gas 1. Cook the small cake for 1½ hours, and the large cake for 2½ hours. Cool in the tins.

Cut the large cake into three horizontal slices. Cut three 2.5 cm (1 inch) slices from the small cake and discard any excess. Leaving one layer of the large cake complete for the base, trim edges of remaining layers to create six decreasing tiers. Place the base cake on the board.

For the tree icing, mix the egg whites and liquid glucose together in a large bowl. Gradually beat in the sifted icing sugar, using hands to knead the mixture when it gets too thick. Knead green food colouring into two-thirds of the icing and wrap the remainder in a polybag to be used later.

Roll out about a quarter of the green icing on a surface lightly dusted with icing sugar to a round 5 cm (2 inches) larger than the base cake. Drape over the cake and smooth sides. Trim off the excess. Position second layer of cake on top. Roll out more icing as before and drape over, letting the icing fall in soft folds around the cake. Repeat with remaining layers. Place a small dome of icing on the top and cover with more icing as before.

Colour small pieces of icing yellow and red. Roll each into a long sausage, twist together and cut into 4 cm (1½ inch) lengths. Bend ends to shape candy canes. Leave on foil or waxed paper to harden overnight.

To make royal icing, beat the egg white and sifted icing sugar together until mixture stands in soft peaks. Put into a piping bag fitted with a large writing nozzle. Pipe on dots of icing and use to secure silver and gold dragees, sugar-coated chocolate buttons and all but one candy cane onto the cake, creating the effect of

Christmas tree decorations.

Pipe on garlands in decorative loops. Leave to harden for at least 2 hours before moving the cake. Dust the cake lightly with sifted icing sugar for a snow effect. Fix the gold star in position on top of the cake.

To make the mice, colour all but a small piece of the reserved tree icing grey, using black food colouring. Shape three plum-sized balls of icing for the bodies and place on foil or waxed paper. Shape three smaller

pieces for the heads. Dampen and secure onto bodies. Shape front limbs, semi-circular feet and ears and fix in place. Roll long pieces of icing for the tails and secure to mice. Fix on dragees for the eyes with dots of royal icing. Brightly colour the remaining tree icing and make into bow ties and hats for the mice.

Arrange mice and small wrapped sweets for presents on the cake board. Give one mouse the remaining candy cane for a walking stick.

CELERY BOATS

Makes about 20
125 g (4 oz) cream cheese
1 tablespoon chives, chopped
1 head of celery, cut into sticks
rice paper
cocktail sticks
few lettuce leaves, shredded
salt and pepper

Put the cheese in a bowl with the chives. Season with salt and pepper and mix well until smooth. Spoon a little of the mixture into each celery stick and spread smoothly. Cut each stick into 6 cm (2½ inch) lengths.

Cut the rice paper into triangular sails, spear with a cocktail stick and press one into each celery boat. Arrange the lettuce on a serving plate and place the celery boats on top.

TUNA TUGS

Makes 24
198 g (7 oz) can tuna fish,
    drained
50 g (2 oz) soft margarine
3 tablespoons mayonnaise
salt and pepper
12 small bridge rolls
¼ cucumber
1 carrot

Put the tuna fish in a bowl and mash with a fork. Add the margarine and mayonnaise and season with salt and pepper. Mix with a fork until smooth. Halve the rolls, place 2 teaspoons of the tuna mixture on each half and smooth to the edges.

Cut the cucumber into 2 cm (1 inch) sticks and place one vertically on each roll. Do the same thing with the carrot to make a funnel.

Make the occasion as Christmassy as you like, use Christmas decorations on the tea table and festive cloths to really set the scene.

MARMITE BITES

Makes about 30
212 g (7½ oz) packet frozen
   puff pastry, thawed
1 tablespoon Marmite
½ teaspoon water

Roll out the pastry thinly on a floured surface into a 25 x 30 cm (10 x 12 inch) rectangle. Mix the Marmite and water together and spread all over the pastry. Roll up loosely from the shorter side like a Swiss roll, with the join underneath. Chill for 20 minutes.

   Cut into 5 mm (¼ inch) slices, arrange on greased baking sheets and make a slit in each from edge to centre. Place in a preheated oven at 200°C, 400°F, Gas 6 for 10 minutes or until golden. Serve warm or cold.

CHEQUERED SANDWICHES

Makes 32 squares
8 slices brown bread
8 slices white bread
Fillings:
50 g (2 oz) butter
6 tablespoons mayonnaise
3 hard-boiled eggs, chopped finely
50 g (2 oz) cream cheese
75 g (3 oz) cheese, grated
2 tablespoons chives, chopped
salt and pepper

For the fillings, beat the butter with the mayonnaise and divide into two bowls. Stir the chopped eggs into one and mix the cheeses and chives into the other. Season with salt and pepper.

   Make the sandwiches using one slice of brown bread, one slice of white bread and one filling for each. Remove the crusts and cut each sandwich into four squares. Arrange them in two layers on a square cake board, alternating the brown and white to create the pattern.

COLA FLOATS

Makes 1.75 litres (3 pints)
1.75 litres (3 pints) cola
12 scoops vanilla ice-cream

Three quarters fill twelve beakers with cola and put a scoop of ice-cream on the top of each. Serve with straws.

Cut out two identical tree shapes from a large piece of green card. Cut shapes from silver foil and coloured paper to decorate. Make a headband from a thin strip of card and attach a star. Hang tree shapes over the child's shoulders with tape or coloured ribbon.

CHOCOLATE NUGGETS

Makes 12
50 g (2 oz) margarine
175 g (6 oz) plain chocolate
2 tablespoons clear honey
250 g (8 oz) digestive biscuits,
 crushed
12 Smarties

Put the margarine, chocolate and honey in a saucepan and heat gently until melted. Stir in the biscuit crumbs and mix thoroughly. Turn into a greased and lined shallow 18 cm (7 inch) square cake tin and smooth the top. Mark into nuggets with a sharp knife and place a Smartie in the centres of each. Leave to set before cutting into nuggets.

GINGERBREAD PEOPLE

Makes 12
125 g (4 oz) plain flour
½ teaspoon bicarbonate of soda
½ teaspoon ground ginger
½ teaspoon ground cinnamon
25 g (1 oz) butter
50 g (2 oz) soft brown sugar
2 tablespoons golden syrup
1 teaspoon milk
50 g (2 oz) icing sugar

Sift the flour, bicarbonate of soda and spices into a bowl. Put the butter, brown sugar and syrup in a pan and heat gently until melted. Cool slightly and mix into the flour with the milk to make a firm dough. Wrap in a polybag and chill 30 minutes.

Turn the dough onto a lightly floured surface and roll out to a 5 mm (¼ - ½ inch) thickness. Using a gingerbread cutter, cut out figures and

All kids love giving and receiving presents. They might like to come to the party dressed as one. Cut two large square shapes and decorate. Fix two straps to the back so the presents hang as shown.

place on greased baking sheets. Place in a preheated oven at 160°C, 325°F, Gas 3 for 10-15 minutes, until firm. Transfer to a wire rack and allow the gingerbread to cool.

Mix the sifted icing sugar with enough water to make a thick glacé icing. Spoon into a piping bag fitted with a fine nozzle and pipe features.

CHERRY MINCE PIES

Makes 12
125 g (4 oz) shortcrust pastry
175 g (6 oz) mincemeat
50 g (2 oz) maraschino cherries,
 drained and quartered
1 teaspoon lemon juice
1 egg white
50 g (2 oz) caster sugar

Roll out the pastry thinly on a lightly floured surface. Stamp out twelve 7.5 cm (3 inch) circles and use to line a bun tin. Prick the bases well and chill for 15 minutes.

Press a piece of foil in each pastry case and place in a preheated oven at 200°C, 400°F, Gas 6 for 10-15 minutes, until the pastry looks set. Remove the foil and return to the oven for a further 2 minutes. Remove from oven and reduce the oven temperature to 180°C, 350°F, Gas 4.

Reserve twelve cherry pieces. Mix the mincemeat, cherries and lemon juice together and divide between the pastry cases.

Whisk the egg white until stiff, then whisk in the sugar a tablespoon at a time. Spoon into a piping bag fitted with a 1 cm (½ inch) fluted nozzle and pipe a rosette on top of each pie. Top with reserved cherry pieces. Return to the oven for 6 minutes, until golden. Serve warm or cold.

HANDY HINTS

PLANNING FOR DIFFERENT AGE GROUPS

You may want a theme party but be unsure of the children's capabilities and what to expect from the age group. In this section, the age groups are broken down into toddlers, children from four to five, six- to ten-year-olds and pre-teens. There is information on what the children in each age group will enjoy doing and ideas for simple food and games.

TODDLERS' PARTIES

Children under three aren't really old enough to appreciate an organized party; they are happy playing amongst themselves. So if you are going to have a party for your toddler have lots of toys and games set out ready for them. The summer is a good time for small children if you have a garden, as they can play outside and make as much mess as they like. But if you are having the party inside, there are several useful tips to bear in mind:

Put away all precious objects, clear low shelves and put the video and answering machine away – there's nothing like a few knobs to twiddle and a video slot for posting things in to attract a small child. Remember that things your family have learned to ignore or leave alone may be items their friends have never seen before.

Keep food very simple Most toddlers will not sit still for very long and will probably end up walking around with food in their hands. So don't let them eat anything messy unless they sit at a table.

Put a safety gate across the stairs to stop children disappearing upstairs. Shut the doors of any rooms you don't want them to go into and lock them if necessary.

Expect the parents to stay as well. Most young children get upset when their parents leave and it's no fun having to cope with weeping and hysterical children at a party. Also they may well be only partly toilet trained and you won't be able to whisk them off to the bathroom and leave other small people on their own. So make it

an occasion for everyone, lay on food and drink for the adults as well and include them in your activities.

Don't ask too many children, two- and three-year-olds usually argue and fight a lot – they invariably want to play with the same toy, and the birthday child might find it difficult to 'share' all his new things. If you keep the numbers small, it won't be such hard work.

Have a mixture of things to do and play with, but don't put them all out at once. Introduce new or different things when toddlers start annoying each other. Have a large cardboard box with a selection of toys inside so the

children can rummage through it or tip everything out. If the party is in the garden, tip a little silver sand, easily obtained from a builder's yard, into a box. Have empty yogurt pots, card-board tubes, toy cars and figures for them to use.

Borrow enough ride-on, or push-along toys from your friends for all the children to have something to play on. It is tricky trying to get them to play together at this age – they will probably stick to their own toys.

Mums with very young children will probably attend parties too, so lay on some food for them as well.

You don't necessarily need invitations – just let the other mums at play-group or the nursery know about the party.

The party is probably best held during a week day. Make it either a coffee morning and just have a small cake and some nibbles, or an early afternoon party, before mums have to rush off to collect older children or get ready for the evening.

FOOD

Keep the food simple for toddlers. Crisps, sausages, small sandwiches and colourful iced cakes are the answer. The children might not want to eat much as they will be busy playing. But the parents will probably appreciate a light snack especially if it has been made with them in mind. Once again keep the food easy – dips and crudités are ideal. Also have plenty of drinks at hand for everyone.

TARAMASALATA

To obtain the desired consistency, you will need a food processor.

Serves 6
5 thin slices white bread
150 ml (¼ pint) water
1 small onion
150 ml (¼ pint) oil
125 g (4 oz) can smoked cod's roe
2 tablespoons lemon juice
1 tablespoon white wine vinegar
salt and pepper

Soak the bread in the water for 10 minutes. Squeeze excess water out of the bread and put into a food processor with the onion and oil. Blend for 30 seconds.

Add remaining ingredients and blend to a smooth dip. Season with salt and pepper and serve with Pitta Bread Fingers. (See page 84.)

HOUMOUS

To obtain the desired consistency, you will need a food processor.

Serves 6
400 g (13 oz) can chickpeas
1 clove garlic, crushed
1 small onion
2 tablespoons tahini (sesame seed paste)
6 tablespoons oil
2-3 teaspoons lemon juice
salt and pepper

Purée the contents of the can of chickpeas in a food processor. Add the garlic, onion and tahini. Add the oil a little at a time, blending until the mixture has the consistency of whipped cream. Add lemon juice and season with salt and pepper. Serve with Pitta Bread Fingers. (See page 84.)

MAYONNAISE DIPS

This recipe incorporates home-made mayonnaise. Alternatively substitute the bought variety and just add the yogurt and herbs.

Serves 6
2 egg yolks
½ teaspoon dried mustard powder
2 tablespoons white wine vinegar
300 ml (½ pint) corn or sunflower oil
1 tablespoon boiling water
4 tablespoons natural yogurt
2 tablespoons parsley, chopped
1 tablespoon chives or spring onions, chopped

Put the egg yolks, mustard and 1 tablespoon of the vinegar in a food processor and blend for a few seconds. While the machine is still running, very gradually trickle in half the oil and then the remaining spoonful of vinegar. Add boiling water. Add the rest of the oil in the same way to make a thick, smooth, creamy consistency. (If the mixture curdles, tip it out, wash the processor bowl and blend another egg yolk in it. Gradually add the curdled mixture to it.) Divide the mayonnaise in half. Add the yogurt to one half and the herbs to the rest. Serve in small dishes with crudités.

CRUDITÉS

½ cucumber
3 carrots
4 sticks celery
1 small red or green pepper, de-seeded
½ cauliflower
bunch of radishes
breadsticks

Wash and trim vegetables and cut into bite-sized pieces about 5 cm (2 inches) long. Break breadsticks into 5 cm (2 inch) lengths. Arrange on platters around the mayonnaise dips.

PINWHEEL SANDWICHES

Makes about 32

4 slices medium sliced brown bread, crusts removed

Filling:

75 g (3 oz) cream cheese

1 tablespoon mayonnaise

1 celery stick

salt and pepper

For the filling, beat the cream cheese with the mayonnaise and salt and pepper to taste.

Cut the celery into four 5 mm (¼ inch) sticks, the same length as the bread. Roll out the bread lightly with a rolling pin and spread thickly with cheese filling. Place a stick of celery across one end of each slice. Roll up tightly, pressing the edge down firmly. Wrap in cling film and chill. Cut the rolls into 1 cm (½ inch) slices to serve.

Try these alternative fillings:

★ peanut butter, Marmite or jam

★ tuna fish mashed with a little mayonnaise and finely chopped cucumber

★ egg mayonnaise and salad cress

★ cheese spreads of various types

★ smooth pâtés, or fish or meat pastes

ICED CAKES

Makes 20

125 g (4 oz) self-raising flour

125 g (4 oz) soft margarine

125 g (4 oz) caster sugar

2 eggs

2-3 drops vanilla essence

20 paper cake cases

Glacé icing:

250 g (8 oz) icing sugar

2-3 tablespoons warm water

food colouring of choice (optional)

To decorate:

glacé cherries

hundreds and thousands

crystallized orange and lemon slices

tiny sweets

Put the flour in a mixing bowl. Add the margarine, sugar, eggs and vanilla essence and beat with wooden spoon until evenly blended.

Using a teaspoon, divide the mixture equally among 20 paper cake cases standing on a baking sheet. Place in a preheated oven at 180°C, 350°F, Gas 4 for 15 minutes, until golden and springy to the touch. Transfer, in the cases, to a wire rack and allow to cool completely.

Mix the sifted icing sugar with enough water to give a smooth coating consistency. Add a few drops of food colouring if liked. Spread the icing over the cakes and decorate with glacé cherries, hundreds and thousands, crystallized orange and lemon slices and tiny sweets to make faces.

Pinwheel sandwiches and iced cakes are ideal for youngsters as they are small, easy to eat and fun to look at.

Four- to Five-Year-Olds

These children have started, or are about to start school and have experienced parties before. They are used to working with other children and sharing toys and games, they get excited about approaching celebrations and look forward to attending.

Invitations are enthusiastically accepted and play an important part in the party.

The birthday child will usually want to invite the whole class, but resist the temptation! Keep numbers to about 12 and try and get someone to help you. While you organize and supervise the games, you need someone else to get the tea ready.

Children of this age group like playing games, especially the more traditional ones – mainly because they know the rules – so include some of those as well as new ones. The children may even have some ideas of their own. Always plan more games than you think you will need – four- to five-year-olds have a short concentration span and play games very quickly.

Pre-plan an activity as they like to make things: start the party with something to make or decorate, like a mask, head-dress or place mat, or finish up with a quiet activity to calm everyone down.

These children can manage their food better, but are still quite clumsy and careless, so ideally sit them down to eat. Decorate the table and have small dishes containing the same things round the table, to save leaning and stretching over everyone. Only pour small amounts of drinks in glasses so there is less to spill, they can always have a top up.

FOOD

BROWNIES

Makes about 16
125 g (4 oz) butter
125 g (4 oz) plain chocolate, broken into pieces
125 g (4 oz) light brown sugar
125 g (4 oz) self-raising flour
pinch of salt
2 eggs, beaten
50 g (2 oz) walnuts, chopped
1-2 tablespoons milk

Grease and base line a 20 cm (8 inch) square cake tin.

Put the butter and chocolate pieces in a bowl over a saucepan of hot, not boiling, water. Stir until melted. Remove the bowl from the heat and stir in the sugar. Leave to cool.

Sift the flour and salt into a mixing bowl and make a well in the centre. Pour in the cooled chocolate mixture. Using a wooden spoon, gradually draw the flour into the liquid, then beat in the eggs and walnuts. Stir well to mix thoroughly and add enough milk to make a soft dropping consistency.

Pour the mixture into the cake tin. Place in a preheated oven at 180°C,

Brownies are popular with children as they are sweet and sticky.

350°F, Gas 4 for about 30 minutes, or until a skewer inserted into the middle of the cake comes out clean. Leave to cool completely in the tin. Cut into squares.

CHEESY SAUSAGE ROLLS

Makes about 24
250 g (8 oz) plain flour
½ teaspoon salt
½ teaspoon dried mustard
   powder
75 g (3 oz) margarine, diced
50 g (2 oz) cheese, grated
2 tablespoons water
250 g (8 oz) sausagemeat
milk to glaze

Sift the flour with the salt and mustard into a bowl. Add the margarine and rub in with fingertips until mixture resembles fine breadcrumbs. Stir in the cheese. Add enough water to make a firm dough. Turn onto a lightly floured surface and knead lightly. Roll out fairly thinly to form a rectangle. Trim edges and cut lengthways into two strips.

Divide the sausagemeat into two equal portions and dust with flour. Shape into two rolls the length of the pastry. Lay one sausagemeat roll on each length of pastry and brush edges with milk. Roll pastry over the meat and seal the edges firmly.

Brush both rolls with more milk and cut into 2.5-4 cm (1-1½ inch) lengths. Arrange on a large baking sheet and place in a preheated oven at 200°C, 400°F, Gas 6 for 15 minutes. Reduce the temperature to 180°C, 350°F, Gas 5 and cook for a further 15 minutes, or until brown.

PEANUT BALLS

Makes 24
250 g (8 oz) full fat soft cheese
2 tablespoons crunchy peanut butter
3 tablespoons fresh breadcrumbs
125 g (4 oz) salted or dry roasted
   peanuts, chopped finely

Using a wooden spoon, beat the cheese and peanut butter together in a bowl until light and fluffy. Stir in the breadcrumbs and mix thoroughly. Use hands to roll the mixture into about 24 small balls.

Roll in the finely chopped peanuts until evenly coated. Chill until ready to serve.

These no-cook cakes are just the thing if you don't have time to bake one yourself. Quick to assemble with bought ingredients they are ideal for busy parents.

ANIMAL BISCUITS

Makes about 50
250 g (8 oz) plain flour
pinch of salt
½ teaspoon dried mustard
  powder
125 g (4 oz) margarine or
  butter, diced
75 g (3 oz) strong cheese,
  grated finely
1 egg yolk
2 tablespoons water
milk, for glazing
sesame seeds to finish

Sift the flour with salt and mustard powder into a bowl. Add the margarine or butter and rub in until mixture resembles fine breadcrumbs. Add the cheese, egg yolk and water and mix with a knife, then your hands to make a firm dough. Turn out onto a lightly floured surface and knead lightly. Wrap in a polybag and chill for 30 minutes.

Roll out the dough to 2 mm (¼ inch) thickness. Use different animal cutters to cut out shapes and place well apart on a greased baking sheet. Brush with milk and sprinkle with sesame seeds.

Place in a preheated oven at 200°C, 400°F, Gas 6 for 15-20 minutes until golden brown. Leave the biscuits to cool for 2 minutes before transferring to a wire rack.

ENGINE CAKE

125 g (4 oz) icing sugar
50 g (2 oz) margarine
2 tablespoons cocoa
To assemble and decorate:
30 cm (12 inch) cake board
4 strips liquorice
9 mini chocolate-covered Swiss rolls
1 extra large chocolate-covered
  Swiss roll
1 large chocolate sponge
  sandwich cake
4 iced fondant cakes
Smarties
chocolate vermicelli
dolly mixtures
1 liquorice Catherine wheel
1 chocolate-covered marshmallow
  biscuit

Make chocolate butter icing by beating the icing sugar, margarine and cocoa together in a bowl. Spread half the icing over the cake board. Arrange two strips of liquorice down the board to make the rails. Put four of the mini rolls across the rails to make the wheels. Cut off a fifth of the extra large Swiss roll and reserve. Put the large piece on top to make the engine.

Put a further two mini rolls across the rails. Cut a square from the chocolate sandwich cake, spread the base with a little butter icing and put on top to make the tender.

Put two more mini rolls at the back of the cake. Cut two rectangles from the remaining sponge cake, spread the base with butter icing and position on top of the mini rolls.

Top both with the iced fondant cakes. Decorate the board with Smarties. Spread a little icing on top of the tender and cover with chocolate vermicelli and dolly mixtures. Stick the Catherine wheel on the front and put the marshmallow biscuit on top of the engine. Place half of the remaining mini roll and the remaining piece of Swiss roll behind. Pipe remaining icing decoratively round the chimney and cab.

BUTTERFLY CAKE

2 x 20 cm (8 inch) round chocolate
  Victoria sponge cakes
Butter icing:
250 g (8 oz) butter
500 g (1 lb) icing sugar
few drops vanilla essence
1-2 tablespoons milk
To assemble and decorate:
250 g (8 oz) apricot jam
2 tablespoons water
25 cm (10 inch) cake board
pink food colouring
small sweets

Beat the butter in a bowl until soft. Gradually beat in the sifted icing sugar, vanilla essence and milk. Use a little of the icing to sandwich the cakes together. Heat the apricot jam and water in a pan until melted. Sieve the jam, return to the pan and bring to the boil. Simmer until mixture is thick enough to coat the back of a spoon. Allow to cool.

Cut the cake in half and position the two halves back to back on the cake board at a slightly slanting angle so the 'wings' are wider apart at the top. Brush the cakes with apricot jam mixture. Coat the top and sides with two-thirds of the butter icing. Tint the remaining icing pink. Put into a piping bag fitted with a fine star nozzle and pipe rosettes round the 'wings'.

Decorate the 'wings' with sweets and leave to set.

SIX- TO TEN-YEAR-OLDS

Children of this age are at school and have been for some time so they are used to being with and playing with other children, especially in organized games. They are the easiest age group to entertain as they are more confident in their skills. They are competitive and like to win but also know how to play as a team. They like energetic games and rushing about, but are also easier to take out than children of younger years. Have a good mixture of games, though, as some won't be as capable with pen and paper as others.

If you live near a park, take the children there so they can play on the swings, have a game of football and play some running-about games.

These children like their food and eat plenty of it! If you give a buffet party, they will load up their plates, usually with all the sweet things, and then leave a lot. It is sometimes easier to serve burgers or hot dogs and oven chips. Make sure you have plenty of tomato sauce!

Games will be appreciated and the group will whizz through them very quickly, so have plenty lined up, even if you don't need them all.

GAMES

RAILWAY CARRIAGE GAME

Collect six newspapers over the week before the party. Juggle the pages around in each one so some are upside-down, some are back to front and so on. Sit six children in two lines opposite each other in a hallway, or somewhere cramped, as if they are in a railway carriage. Ask them to rearrange the paper and put it back in the right order. This causes the most amazing amount of chaos and much laughing! The first one to put the paper back correctly is the winner.

BALLOON TREASURE HUNT

Write the clues on small pieces of paper and insert them into balloons before blowing them up. Each clue should lead to a pencil which is used to pop the next balloon which contains another clue. Pencil number 1 pops balloon number 1 which

Cut fishy shapes from thin paper and line up the children. Ask them to Flap the Fish down the racecourse with a rolled-up newspaper, first one to the end wins!

contains the clue to find pencil number 2 which in turn pops balloon number 2. Ask the children to work in pairs as it's much more fun having someone to work out clues with. Have a balloon at each stage for each couple but only one at the end for the winners to pop and find the clue to the hidden treasure.

GIANT'S NECKLACE

Have six cotton reels, a length of wool and a pair of rubber gloves for each team. Divide the children into two teams. The first player must rush up to one set of cotton reels and after putting on the rubber gloves they must thread the reels onto the wool. Once completed they must slip them off again and run back to their team. The next player then has a go. The first team whose players have all had a turn and returned to their group wins.

FLOUR MOUNTAIN

Tightly pack a pudding basin with flour and invert it on a plate. Stand the plate on a piece of newspaper. Lift off the basin and place a small sweet on top of the flour and a spoon by the side. Each player must take it in turns to scoop away a spoonful of flour and put it in an empty bowl. Whoever is responsible for the sweet falling must put his hands behind his back and pick the sweet up with his mouth! Put the flour back in the basin and play again.

SMELL THAT!

Collect up things that have a distinctive smell, like coffee, mints, lemon juice, soap and so on and arrange them on a tray. Keep the objects out of sight and smell of the children. Blindfold the children and take one of the objects round so they can all smell it without speaking. When everyone has had a sniff, ask them if they recognize it. The first person to guess correctly wins and receives a small prize.

FOOD

Keep the food fairly simple; six- to ten-year-olds are probably happiest with burgers and chips and plenty of drinks! But to create a party mood have some nibbles around, too.

SPIKY HEDGEHOGS

Makes about 50
2 oranges or grapefruits
150 g (5 oz) cheese, cubed
225 g (8 oz) can pineapple pieces, drained
50 cocktail sticks
2 stuffed olives, halved crossways
1 small gherkin, halved
20 cocktail sausages, grilled

Cut a slice off the base of each fruit so it will stand up.

Spear the cheese and pineapple with cocktail sticks and stick into one of the fruits to make the spines.

Pierce 2 olive halves and 1 gherkin piece with halved cocktail sticks. Push

Arrange the food in interesting and different ways to make it more appealing to the partygoers!

into the fruit to make eyes and nose.

Pierce the sausages with the remaining cocktail sticks and press into the other fruit. Make the eyes and nose with the 2 olive halves and 1 gherkin as before.

ORANGE & PINEAPPLE DRINK

Makes 2 litres (3½ pints)
4 oranges
50 g (2 oz) caster sugar
1.2 litres (2 pints) boiling water
600 ml (1 pint) pineapple juice
orange slices to decorate.

Finely grate the rind from the oranges and place in a heatproof jug. Add the sugar and the water and stir until dissolved. Squeeze the juice from the oranges and add to the jug. Cool and then add the pineapple juice.

Chill and serve topped with orange slices.

Buffets are more relaxing for older children as boys and girls get easily embarrassed if they have to sit next to one another.

together with the raspberry purée and cream layer in the centre. Spread the rest of the cake with the remaining cream and then press the flaked almonds over the sides. Pipe rosettes of cream round the top edges and chill until needed.

If using a fresh peach, place the sugar and lemon juice and a little water in a pan and stir over a gentle heat until the sugar dissolves. Add the peach slices and cook for 3 minutes. Remove with a slotted spoon and drain on kitchen paper. Chill.

Arrange the peach slices down the centre of the cake and drizzle a little of the remaining raspberry purée over each slice. Decorate with the reserved raspberries.

PEACH MELBA CAKE

The fresh peach, sugar and lemon juice in the topping can be substituted with 8 slices of canned peaches.

2 eggs
50 g (2 oz) caster sugar
few drops vanilla essence
50 g (2 oz) plain flour
Topping:
250 g (8 oz) raspberries, thawed
  if frozen
3 tablespoons caster sugar
300 ml (½ pint) double cream
2 tablespoons milk
50 g (2 oz) flaked almonds, toasted
1 fresh peach, stoned and sliced
2 tablespoons caster sugar
1 tablespoon lemon juice

Grease and line an 18 cm (7 inch) square cake tin. Whisk the eggs, sugar and vanilla essence in a bowl until

thick and pale. Sift half the flour into the mixture and fold it in, using a large metal spoon. Sift and fold in the remaining flour.

Pour into cake tin and place in a preheated oven at 190°C, 375°F, Gas 5 for 20-30 minutes until well risen and golden and a skewer inserted into the centre comes out clean. Allow to cool slightly in the tin and then turn onto a wire rack to cool completely.

Trim edges and cut in half crossways. Reserve half the raspberries for decoration but press the rest through a sieve into a bowl. Stir in the caster sugar. Spread three quarters of the purée on one half of the cake.

Whip the cream and milk together until the mixture forms soft peaks. Place one third in a piping bag fitted with a medium star nozzle and set aside. Spread one third of the remaining cream over both halves of the cake, then sandwich the two

LEMON SURPRISE CAKE

175 g (6 oz) butter or margarine
175 g (6 oz) caster sugar
4 teaspoons lemon rind
6 tablespoons lemon juice
3 eggs
175 g (6 oz) self-raising flour, sifted
Filling:
25 g (1 oz) butter or margarine
25 g (1 oz) demerara sugar
25 g (1 oz) Brazil nuts, chopped
  finely
75 g (3 oz) sultanas
25 g (1 oz) glacé cherries
4 teaspoons lemon rind
¼ teaspoon grated nutmeg
To decorate:
icing sugar, sifted
sugared lemon halves

Grease and base line an 18 cm (7 inch) round cake tin. Cream the butter or margarine and sugar in a mixing bowl until light and fluffy. Add the lemon rind. Beat the lemon juice with the eggs and stir half into the creamed mixture. Fold in half the sifted flour and then add the remaining egg mixture and then the rest of the flour. Spoon half the mixture into the tin.

To make the filling, melt the butter or margarine in a small saucepan, add sugar and stir until it has dissolved. Remove from heat and stir in the nuts, sultanas, glacé cherries, lemon rind and nutmeg.

Sprinkle half of the filling mixture over the sponge mixture in the tin. Spoon remaining sponge mix over that and sprinkle with remaining filling mix. Place the cake in a pre-heated oven at 180°C, 350°F, Gas 4 for 1¼-1½ hours until risen and golden and a skewer inserted into the centre of the cake comes out clean. Cover with foil towards the end of the

baking time to prevent the top from burning. Cool for 5 minutes in the tin, then turn onto a wire rack to cool completely.

Dredge with sifted icing sugar and decorate with sugared lemon halves.

Impress your guests by having a centre-piece, like a Peach Melba or Lemon Suprise Cake, on the party table.

PRE-TEENS

Once pre-teen children start secondary school they feel very mature and grown-up. They may not want a party for various reasons which they may not offer – sometimes they feel embarrassed about having to ask the opposite sex. So you may find you have to approach parties for pre-teens in a different way.

Try a sleep-over for a change. Ask your child to ask three or four of their friends to stay the night. They must bring some bedding and their pyjamas and arrive a little later in the evening. This usually means giving up the lounge so they can bed down on the floor watching videos all night while they discuss members of the opposite sex. Provide some nibbles but nothing too messy – think of their bedding and your carpet!. Be prepared, too, to call downstairs at three in the morning to ask them to be a little quieter!

Another idea is to allow a small group of friends to cook something simple for themselves to eat. You must keep a discreet eye on them of course!

If it is warm and sunny and you have a tent or can borrow one from a friend, they might like to have a party in the garden and sleep out there, too

Lots of older children like the informality of discos and dislike being organized into playing games. It is best to book a hall for a disco as they are very noisy to have at home. Choose a venue that isn't too big – a large empty space will discourage people from dancing. You could share the costs with one or two friends whose children have birthdays about the same time – their friends will also increase the numbers and fill the place up a bit. You will definitely need help, though, especially if the party is in the evening. You will need some men on the door to prevent unwelcome guests from entering and to make sure everyone leaves the premises safely. Provide buffet food and drinks so people can help themselves when they aren't dancing. A good DJ will organize the kids well and even sort out some games, leaving you free to set out food and drinks.

Have a fancy dress party: this makes older children more relaxed and everyone will love dressing up.

Taking pre-teens out is a much more orderly affair. They are usually quite sensible, especially if they are all the same sex and are confident of their abilities. Take them swimming, roller-skating or bowling, then out for a burger or back home for a meal you have prepared earlier. What they do and where they eat will depend on the maturity of your child and his or her friends. If you are taking out more than four children you will need a friend to come along to help with the organization and transport.

Pre-teens are old enough to help in the preparation of their parties.

GARLIC BREAD
Serves 20
1 large French loaf
175 g (6 oz) butter, softened
2 cloves garlic, crushed
1 tablespoon parsley, chopped
salt and pepper

★ Make diagonal cuts 2.5 cm (1 inch) apart, slicing three-quarters of the way through the French loaf.
★ Cream together the butter, garlic, parsley, salt and pepper until thoroughly mixed. Spread liberally between the slices and spread any remaining butter over the top.
★ Wrap in foil and place in a preheated oven at 200°C, 400°F, Gas 6 for 10 minutes. Draw back the foil and expose the top of the loaf and cook for a further 5-10 minutes, until crisp.
★ Remove foil, cut through each slice and serve hot.

FOOD

These recipes are useful if you are planning to entertain a large number of children from this age group. There are also suggestions for some more adventurous dishes which are suitable for smaller numbers.

PARTY PIZZA

Serves 18 to 24
500 g (1 lb) plain flour
1 teaspoon salt
7 g (¼ oz) dried yeast
1 teaspoon sugar
300 ml (½ pint) warm water
2 tablespoons oil
Topping:
3 tablespoons oil
3 large onions, chopped
3 x 397 g (13 oz) cans chopped
    tomatoes, drained
2 teaspoons oregano
salt and pepper
3 tablespoons tomato purée
500 g (1 lb) mozzarella cheese,
    sliced thinly
2 x 50 g (1¾ oz) cans anchovy fillets,
    drained and halved lengthways
18 black olives

Sift the flour and salt together in a large bowl. Dissolve the yeast and sugar in a little of the water and leave in a warm place for 10 minutes. Add to the flour with the remaining water and oil. Mix to a soft dough.

Turn onto a floured surface and knead for 10 minutes until smooth and elastic. Place in a clean bowl, cover and leave in a warm place for about 1½ hours, until the dough has doubled in size.

For the topping, heat the oil in a pan, add onions and fry until softened. Add the tomatoes and oregano and season with salt and pepper. Cook for 5 minutes and leave to cool.

Turn the dough onto a floured surface and knead for a few minutes. Divide into three pieces and roll each into a 25 cm (10 inch) circle and place on greased baking sheets. Spread 1 tablespoon of tomato purée over each dough round. Divide the tomato mixture between the rounds and cover with cheese. Arrange the anchovies and olives on top of each one.

Place in a preheated oven at 200°C, 400°F, Gas 6 for 15-20 minutes until golden brown and bubbling. Serve immediately.

Pizza and garlic bread are both popular with older children and perfect for parties. as they can be prepared earlier and heated up when needed They can even be made and frozen beforehand.

POTATO & DILL SALAD

Serves 20
1.75 kg (4 lb) new potatoes
pinch of salt
4 tablespoons French dressing
6-8 spring onions
4 dill cucumbers
300 ml (½ pint) mayonnaise
4 tablespoons natural yogurt

Cook the potatoes in their skins in boiling salted water for about 15 minutes, until just tender. Drain and remove the skins. Cut potatoes into large cubes and put into a bowl. Add the French dressing, toss lightly and leave to cool. Slice the onions and cucumbers thinly and add to the potatoes.

Mix the mayonnaise and yogurt until smooth. Add to the salad and toss well. Transfer to bowls and serve.

LAMB & VEGETABLE KEBABS

Serves 4

500 g (1 lb) lean lamb, cubed
4 cherry tomatoes, or 2 small
    tomatoes, halved
8 button mushrooms
1 green pepper, de-seeded
    and cut into squares
2 tablespoons olive oil
freshly cooked rice to serve
lemon slices to garnish

Divide the lamb, tomatoes, mushrooms and pepper into four equal portions and thread them onto greased skewers, alternating the ingredients.

Brush a little oil over the kebabs and place them under a preheated moderate grill for about 12-15 minutes, turning occasionally, until all ingredients are cooked. Brush the meat with olive oil from time to time while cooking.

Serve kebabs on a bed of rice, garnished with lemon slices.

STUFFED MUSHROOMS

Makes 8

8 large cup mushrooms
½ onion, chopped finely
25 g (1oz) fresh white breadcrumbs
175 g (6 oz) sausagemeat
1 tablespoon parsley, chopped
½ teaspoon dried mixed herbs
salt and pepper
25 g (1 oz) butter or margarine, diced
To garnish:
2 tablespoons sweetcorn kernels
tomato quarters

Remove the stalks from the mushrooms and chop finely. Put the stalks,

Older children are more adventurous in their tastes so try out some Stuffed Mushrooms and Lamb and Vegetable Kebabs.

onion, breadcrumbs, sausagemeat, parsley and dried herbs in a bowl. Season with salt and pepper and mix together well.

Place the mushroom caps rounded side down in a greased ovenproof dish. Spoon the stuffing mixture into the mushroom caps and dot the butter over the top. Place in a preheated oven at 190°C, 375°F, Gas 5 for about 25 minutes until the stuffing is cooked right through. Garnish with the sweetcorn and tomatoes. Serve hot.

SWIMMING POOL CAKE

275 g (9 oz) self-raising flour
25 g (1 oz) cocoa
1 teaspoon baking powder
5 eggs
300 g (10 oz) soft margarine
300 g (10 oz) caster sugar
Butter icing:
175 g (6 oz) butter
300 g (10 oz) icing sugar, sifted
25 g (1 oz) cocoa
2 teaspoons boiling water
Glacé icing:
375 g (12 oz) icing sugar
4 tablespoons water
To assemble and decorate:
30 cm (12 inch) square cake board
2 x 250 g (8 oz) packets ready-to-roll
   icing
cornflour for dusting
blue, red, pink and yellow food
   colourings
2 x 150 g (5 oz) bars milk chocolate
red or black liquorice bootlace

Two days ahead roll out a little of the
ready-to-roll icing on a surface dusted

MAKING THE SWIMMING POOL CAKE

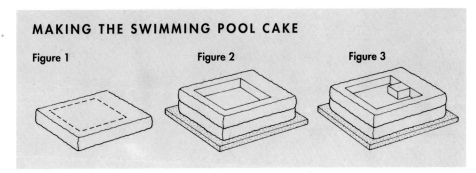

Figure 1   Figure 2   Figure 3

with cornflour to a rectangle 7.5 x 3 cm (3 x 1¾ inches). Mark lines along the surface of the diving board and leave to harden for two days on a piece of non-stick baking parchment.

To make the cake, grease and line two 28 x 18 cm (11 x 7 inch) shallow tins. Sift the flour, cocoa and baking powder into a large bowl. Add the eggs, margarine and sugar and beat until smooth. Spoon into the tins and place in a preheated oven, 180°C, 350°F, Gas 4 for 25 minutes. Turn onto a wire rack and leave to cool.

Colour an egg-sized piece of ready-to-roll icing pink. To make the boy, roll a small piece to a flattened sausage shape. Cut the arms and legs . Pull out the limbs and shape with your fingers. Position a ball of icing for the head . Use a cocktail stick to mark the navel. Shape another ball of icing to make the girl's head, and a separate arm, waving. Mark the fingers with a knife . For the diver, shape two legs and leave to harden.

Beat the butter, sifted icing sugar, cocoa and water together until smooth to make the buttercream. Place one cake on the board. Cut an 18 x 12.5 cm (7 x 5 inch) rectangle out of the centre of the second cake (see figure 1). Cut a small square from this spare rectangle to make the diving board base. Place the cake 'frame' over the cake on the board, sandwiching them together with butter icing (see figure 2).

Reserve a small piece of the ready-to-roll icing for the towels and other trimmings, and colour the rest blue. Roll out thinly and place in the

hollow of the cake to make the water.

Reserve 3 tablespoons of the butter icing. Use the remainder to smooth over the top and sides of the cake. Use the chocolate bars to cover the top of the cake, cutting with a hot knife where necessary.

Sift the icing sugar into a bowl, add water and beat until smooth to make the glacé icing. Place 1 tablespoon of the glacé icing in a small piping bag fitted with a plain nozzle, and reserve. Colour the remainder blue. Use a little to make puddles round the tiled edge, then spoon the remainder into the centre of the pool. Use a cocktail stick to pull the icing towards the sides of the pool to make the ripples.

Shape the reserved ready-to-roll icing into a rubber ring and the towels. Place them around the pool.

Stick diving board base (see figure 3) to the cake using a little of the reserved butter icing. Put the diving board in position and fix in place using more icing. Arrange the swimmers in the pool.

Paint the rubber ring, towels and swimmers using the food colourings. Use the reserved icing in the bag to outline the ripples round the edge of the pool and round the swimmers . Pipe the remaining buttercream to make the hair.

Cut two small lengths of liquorice bootlace and bend to shape the hand rails of the pool. Press one end into the water and the other into the chocolate to hold securely in position. (Use a hot skewer to make a hole in the chocolate tiles, if necessary.)

★★★ ACKNOWLEDGEMENTS ★★★

Lupe A Cunha 2A, 73, 82A

The Susan Griggs Agency/Sandra Lousada 10, 11, 12/3, 13

OCTOPUS PUBLISHING GROUP LTD;
Mick Duff 20/1, 43, 44/5, 68, 69, 70/1, 82/3 Alan Duns 60/1, 84A, 85B, 86A, 86/7, 91, 94
James Jackson 36 Chris Knaggs 37, 62 Duncan McNicol 72 Michael Michaels 59
Paul Williams 6/7, 18/9, 19, 22, 23A, 23B, 28, 29, 30, 30/1, 47, 61, 63, 76, 77A, 78, 84B, 89, 92, 93

THE FOLLOWING PICTURES WERE PROVIDED BY FAMILY CIRCLE;
23, 27, 35, 49, 50A, 50B, 51, 52, 52/3, 53, 54/5, 67, 74, 75, 85A, 90, 94/5

SPECIAL PHOTOGRAPHY BY FIONA PRAGOFF

1, 2 (right), 6, 14/5, 16, 17, 18, 24, 25, 26, 31, 32, 33, 34A, 34B, 38, 39A, 39B, 40, 41, 42, 46, 48, 56, 57, 58, 60, 64, 65, 66A, 66B, 77B, 79, 80/1, 88

Special thanks to Ginny Duhanes, Claire Worthington and Louise Cooper
for assistance and help with the styling.